THE MINIONS MOOR

The author & publisher are
both members of

THE MINIONS MOOR

A Guide to South-East Bodmin Moor, Cornwall

by

Peter Stanier

All rights reserved. No part of this publication may be reproduced or transmitted in any form or by any means, electronic or mechanical, including photocopying, recording, or any information storage and retrieval system, without permission from the publisher.

First Edition published June, 1986.
Enlarged, Second Edition published December 1996.
© Peter Stanier
Designed by Toni Carver
Produced, printed & published by
The St. Ives Printing & Publishing Company
High Street, St. Ives, Cornwall.

ISBN 0 948385 29 4

Cover Photograph: Craddock Moor Mine by the author.

CONTENTS

List of Illustrations	6
Introduction	9
The Four Moors	11
1. Cheesewring Moor	13
2. Craddock Moor	29
3. Caradon Moor	37
4. Kilmar Moor	45
Geology	51
Landforms and Landscape	52
Archaeology	57
Tin Streaming	63
Early Mining	64
The Mining Boom	67
Mineworkers	72
Mining Villages	73
Postscript: 20th Century Mining	75
Water and Water Power	79
A Mining Glossary	81
Railways	87
Moorstone Cutting	91
Granite Quarrying	95
Daniel Gumb	101
Boundary Stones and Markers	105
Rock Climbing	109
The Cheesewring and Wilkie Collins	113
Further Reading	117
Index	119

LIST OF ILLUSTRATIONS

Maps and Plans

Bodmin Moor 10
The Four Moors 11
The walk across Cheesewring Moor 14
Plan of Stowe's Pound 21
Layout of buildings at Prince of Wales Shaft 23
The walk across Craddock Moor 28
Bronze Age hut-circles and fields on Craddock Moor 31
The walk across Caradon Moor 36
The walk across Kilmar Moor 44
Simplified geology 50
Prehistoric sites 56
Clanacombe and Stowe's sections of Cornwall Great United Mine 66
Mines and railways in 1845 (N. Whitley) 68
South Caradon Mine 70
Marke Valley Mine 71
Workings along main lode of Phoenix United Mine 82
Liskeard & Caradon Railway and its branches 88
Railway mania at Minions 89
Developments at Cheesewring Quarry, 1870-1980 96
Daniel Gumb's House (J. Coode) 102

Photographs

Stone cist of the Rillaton Barrow 15
The Cheesewring and Stowe's Hill 24
Pumping engine house at Prince of Wales Shaft 25
The Hurlers 26
The Hurlers and South Phoenix Mine 26
Picnic time on the Cheesewring (S. Bramble) 27
Prince of Wales Shaft, Phoenix United Mine 27
Engine houses at West Phoenix Mine in 1938 (H.G. Ordish) 33
Minions Cross, or Long Tom 33

Hut-circle on Craddock Moor	34
Craddock Moor field system	34
Craddock Moor Mine	35
Ruins at Sump Shaft, South Caradon Mine	38
Salisbury Shaft, Marke Valley Mine	42
Rule's Shaft, South Caradon Mine	42
Prehistoric field systems at Sharp Tor	46
Three cairns atop Langstone Downs	48
Bearah Tor Quarry	48
Sharptor from Phoenix United Mine (S. Bramble)	49
The Cheesewring	53
Cairn circle and cist at Kilmar Tor	58
The Pipers standing stones at the Hurlers	59
Hut-circle on Craddock Moor	60
Old turf steed above the Witheybrook Marsh	62
Cow and the Witheybrook tinworks pond	64
Minions in the early twentieth century	73
Minions Primitive Methodist Chapel	74
Crow's Nest Chapel	74
Houseman's engine house in 1969	76
Sinking the Prince of Wales Shaft, c.1910	77
Shallow workings for tin at Silver Valley in 1936 (H.G. Ordish)	78
Round buddle at East Caradon Mine	83
Grooves cut in a moorstone below the Cheesewring	92
Shaped and abandoned moorstone west of Cheesewring	94
Cheesewring Quarry in about 1910	97
East Cornwall Bank (now Barclays) at Liskeard	98
Splitting a granite block at Bearah Quarry	99
Daniel Gumb's House today	103
Moorstone carvings near Cheesewring Cottages	104
Carved boundary symbols at Cheesewring Quarry (2 photographs)	106
Carved boundary number on a rock at Bearah Tor (J. Berry)	107
Boundary stone on Cheesewring Moor	108

Eyefull Tower 110
Khyber Wall 111
Sport Climbing 112

Sketches

The Rillaton Gold Cup (inset) 15
Moorstones on Cheesewring Moor 16
Daniel Gumb's Cave 18
The Cheesewring 19
Summit rocks, Stowe's Hill 22
Stowe's Hill before quarrying commenced (J. Allen) 20
Granite posts at Gold Diggings Quarry 30
Silver Valley engine house 32
Minions Cross (inset) 33
Rule's Shaft, South Caradon Mine 39
LCR milepost on Caradon Hill 40
LCR boundary post at Gonamema 40
Stamps engine at work, Wheal Jenkin 41
Gonamena 43
Boundary Stones 46
Fleur-de-lis carvings at Cheesewring, Bearah and Kilmar 47
The leaning western rock at Kilmar Tor (J. Allen) 54
Summit tors on Stowe's Hill 55
Wheal Jenkin engine house as drawn in 1837 65
Beam engine for pumping 81
Beam engine for winding 81
Horse whim round at Webb's Shaft, South Caradon Mine 84
'The Cheese Wring near Liskeard' (J. Allen) 114
The Cheesewring, from an old print 114

Unless otherwise stated, all illustrations are by the author

INTRODUCTION

THIS is an introductory guide to the important natural and man-made features on south-east Bodmin Moor. It is for the casual visitor and those with more time to spare, and will have succeeded if they are helped to see things in a new way, enriching their appreciation of this fascinating landscape with the pleasure felt by the author.

This present volume is a much enlarged and revised edition of the first guide published in 1986. During the intervening decade the moor has seen an increasing number of visitors, in addition to the designation of a Minions Heritage Area by Caradon District Council, a major archaeological survey undertaken by the Cornwall Archaeological Unit, the construction of new car parks at each end of Minions village, the opening of the Minions Heritage Centre in a converted landmark engine house, and the conservation of the buildings around the Prince of Wales Shaft on the Phoenix United Mine.

I have chosen to keep the descriptions of four moorland walks in their original brief form (with minor amendments), but more information has been added elsewhere as a source of reference to be read at leisure before, during or after setting foot on the moor. The book does not pretend to be comprehensive, but intends to be a useful summary, explaining a little more about the features of the moor, what to see and how to look. A selected reading list indicates follow-up research.

The Minions Moor (my term) is readily accessible, just a few miles by road to the north of Liskeard. It is well known for the Cheesewring rocks and offers the scenic beauty of the moors, with far-reaching views in all directions. This is a high part of Bodmin Moor, much being over 300 m. The going is generally good on the open moor, with several well defined tracks or paths in the vicinity of Minions. Boggy ground can dry hard during the summer months, but should be treated with respect in winter. The moorland weather varies from the extremes of hot, cloudless skies, with hardly a breath of wind, to thick, swirling mists and driving rain. The latter in no way detracts from the unique character of the district, and does much to emphasise the close relationship between moor and climate. The treeless landscape testifies that the wind is seldom still; where they have gained a foothold, stunted hawthorns lean alarmingly away from the prevailing wind.

For its size, the Minions Moor is arguably one of the richest possible areas, offering much for those with an interest in archaeology, industrial archaeology, geology, geography or natural history. Archaeological remains belong notably to the Bronze Age: the Hurlers and Craddock Moor stone circles, various cairns and barrows (including the Rillaton Barrow) and traces of field systems and hut-circles. The whole is overlooked by the stone-walled fortress of Stowe's Pound, now believed to be of Neolithic date. Extractive industries have had the greatest impact on the moors and left the most obvious remains – tin-streaming (probably worked since Bronze Age times) and deep mining for tin and copper. The great mining boom covered about fifty years, from the discovery of rich copper lodes at South Caradon Mine in 1836. Some activity continued until the last important mine closed in 1914. There was also granite cutting and quarrying. The products of the mines and quarries were carried on the Liskeard & Caradon Railway (built 1844-6) to Moorswater near Liskeard, and thence to Looe for shipment. With the failure of the mines, the railway closed at the end of 1916, but its various moorland branches can be traced with relative ease. Many of the surrounding villages owe their development to the mining boom of the mid-nineteenth century, and there are good examples of workers' cottages where they have escaped modernisation.

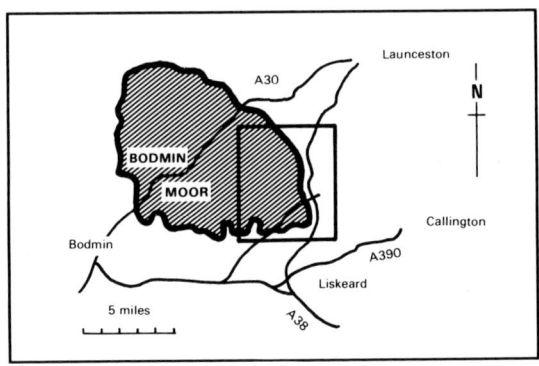

THE FOUR MOORS

MOST of the area of the Minions Moor falls within the parishes of Linkinhorne and St Cleer, with a small part in North Hill. There are four parts, called here for convenience, the Cheesewring, Craddock, Caradon and Kilmar Moors. The main features of each moor are described, based on a recommended walking route with hints of further diversions. The walks are intended to give an introductory guide only – the reader is by no means bound to follow them! Many variations can be made and there is little problem of getting lost in

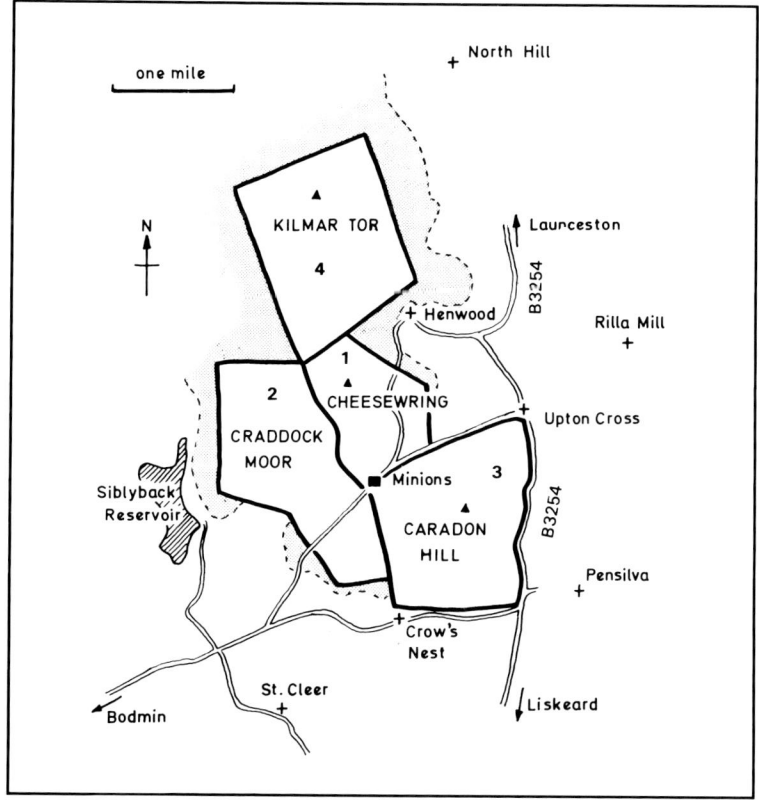

such small areas. The bird's-eye location maps for each moor should be adequate, but further reference can be made to the Ordnance Survey 1:50000 Landranger map 201 (Plymouth and Launceston) and the more detailed 1:25000 scale maps, the Pathfinder 1339 (Bodmin Moor East) or the Explorer map 9 (Bodmin Moor); the extreme southern part of the moor is found on Pathfinder map 1348 (Liskeard).

MINIONS is the best centre for exploring this part of Bodmin Moor, but other access points are noted in the text. Minions is the highest village in Cornwall, at 300 m above sea level. Many of the terraced cottages were built for miners and their families in the 1850s and 1860s, while the railway once crossed the road in the middle of the village – small wonder that it was once known as Cheesewring Railway. The present name derives from Minions Mound, a barrow (once much larger) at the west end of the village. The former Primitive Methodist Chapel of 1863 was built at the height of mining activity, but at one time Minions boasted another chapel, as well as the Cheesewring Hotel and a temperance hotel. Walking is the recommended means of travel, and all routes can begin in the centre of the village.

Note: All the moorland is privately owned, although there are large areas of common land and walkers have had relatively free access for many years. The routes described should not imply they are public rights of way. Please respect this, do not worry livestock and close all gates.

1. CHEESEWRING MOOR
(Minimum 2½ miles or 3.6 km)

THIS is the smallest and most popular of the four moors, mostly visited for the Hurlers and Cheesewring rocks, yet its size belies an astonishing variety of features. Step out of Minions on the St Cleer road (to the west), turning immediately right past the car park onto the moor to follow a signposted track to the *Hurlers* (1). There are three stone circles here, up to 43 m diameter; several stones are fallen or missing, and the south circle has only two left standing. This monument is in the care of English Heritage, but managed by the Cornwall Heritage Trust. It dates from about 1500 BC, towards the end of the Early Bronze Age, but we shall never know what rituals or ceremonies took place here, or at similar circles in Cornwall, although the site on a gently sloping crest of the moor may be significant. There is a fanciful tradition that the Hurlers were 'men changed into stones because they profaned the Lord's day by throwing a ball' (Hurling was a sport once common in Cornwall). Just to the west are two *standing stones* (2), apparently related to the circles or two players who attempted to escape the vengeance from heaven?

Nearby in a gully are two *granite obelisks* (3), carved 'RIL 1846' and numbered '6' and '7'. There are at least ten of these boundary stones, erected to define the bounds of the Duchy of Cornwall's Rillaton Manor. A short walk north finds one in the *Witheybrook tin works* (4), a deep gully with a pond anciently excavated for tin-bearing gravels and emptying into the Witheybrook Marsh, itself worked for alluvial tin on many occasions.

It is possible to reach the Cheesewring and Stowe's Hill from here, but it may be better to reserve further investigation for the Craddock Moor route (walk 2). Instead, almost directly in line with the Hurlers, and just visible on the skyline, is a large burial mound or 'tumulus'. This is the Rillaton Barrow (5) in which a famous corrugated gold cup was found in 1837. Dating from about 1500 BC, the Rillaton Gold Cup is only 8.25 cm high. It is displayed in the British Museum, although a copy is in the Royal Cornwall Museum at Truro. The

THE WALK ACROSS CHEESEWRING MOOR.

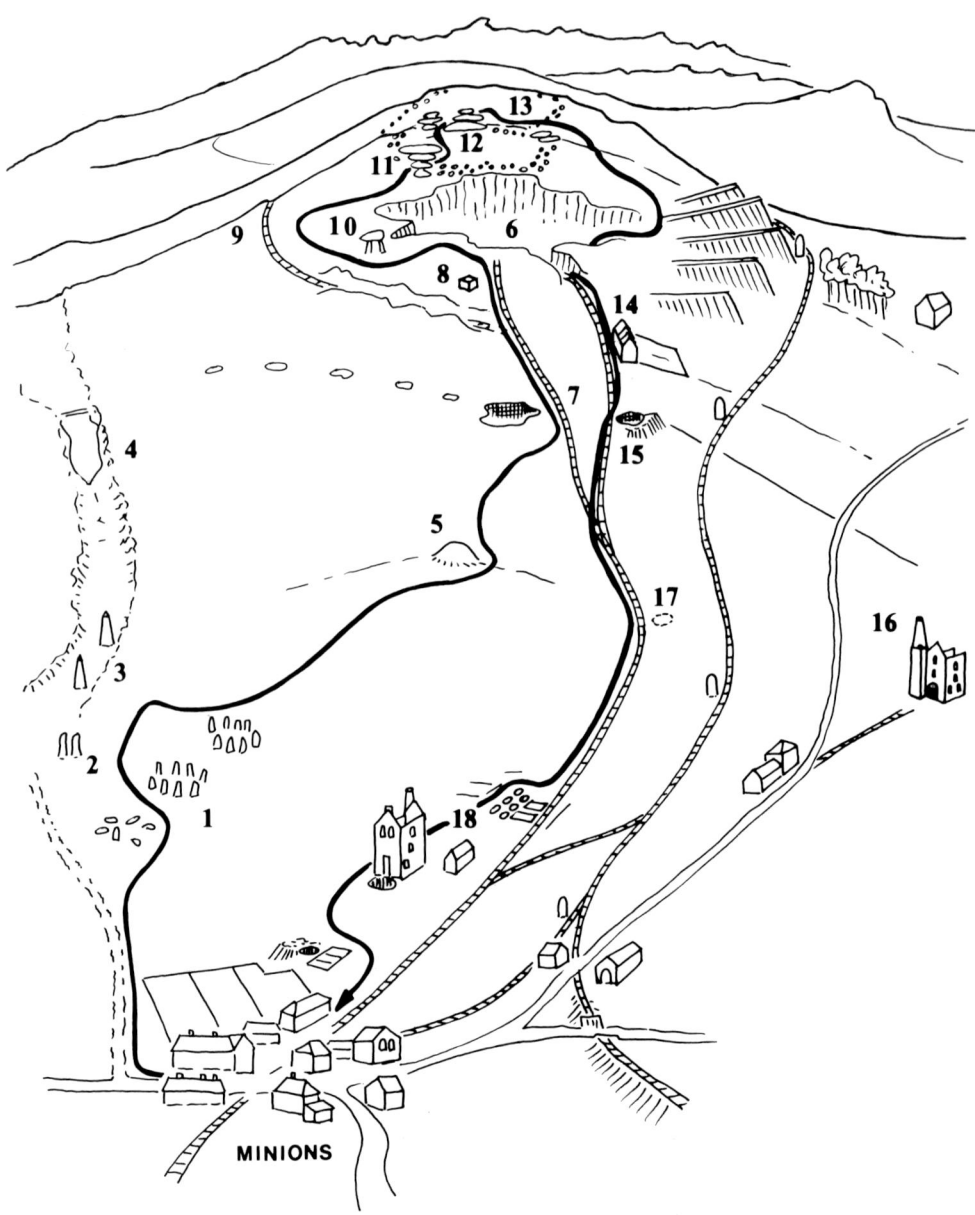

The stone cist of the Rillaton Barrow, from which the famous gold cup was recovered in 1837. Sketch: The Rillaton Cup.

centre of the barrow has been robbed by a deep excavation, but the restored stone 'cist' in which the cup was found is at the east end of the mound. The barrow is well-sited atop a low hill which provides a good viewpoint.

The route crosses many surface workings by the 'Old Men', mainly for tin. Long lines of overgrown pits and mounds follow mineral lodes trending west-east, named in order from Minions: the Prosper, Grace Dieu, Greenhill, Shelstone and Phoenix Lodes. The fenced shafts along this last, major lode are passed before reaching Stowe's Hill, the south slope of which is scarred by the deep **Cheesewring Quarry** (6). From just below the fence around the enormous collapse at Anne's New Engine Shaft on the Phoenix Lode, the granite sleeper blocks of the **Liskeard & Caradon Railway** (7) are well preserved and can be followed to the quarry edge. On the left are the thick walls of the quarry's ruined ***powder magazine*** (8). The quarry was begun when the railway was built in 1844-6, but when workings were deepened in 1871, a new branch was made at a lower level to enter through a cutting. Traces of sidings and other features could be seen until the spring of 1984, when the quarry interior and waste tips were devastated in the search for stone to repair a breakwater at Plymouth. The waste tips on the downhill side of the quarry were once the most

MOORSTONES

The moorstones which scatter the moor are a frequent reminder of the area's industrial past.

A moorstone split by 'Plugs and Feathers.'

Moorstone with marks for 'wedge and groove' cutting.

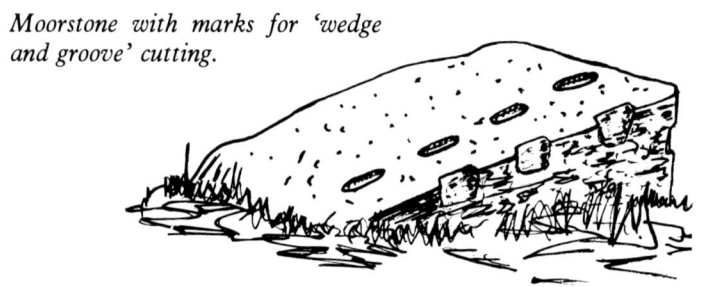

An abandoned moorstone near the Cheesewring.

impressive of their type in Cornwall, with level tops along which large angular waste stones were trammed. Although their original form has been ruined, their area still gives an indication of their scale – only the best granite was sought.

The fine silver-grey granite was used mainly for engineering and architectural work. It was sent by rail to Looe and thence by sea to public works in London and elsewhere. Nineteenth-century contracts included granite for Devonport Dockyard, docks from Birkenhead to Copenhagen, breakwaters at Alderney and Dover, the Spithead forts, Thames Embankment, Westminster and Tower bridges, and a lighthouse in Ceylon. For most of its history, the quarry was worked by John Freeman & Sons, who had over 80 quarries in Cornwall. At its peak in the late 1860s, over 100 men and boys were employed here, but decline in trade and the inability to quarry beneath the protected Cheesewring meant that there was little work here after the Great War. For a number of years there remained at least three large timber cranes, supported by wire guys slung across the quarry opening and anchored at its edges.

The vertical and horizontal joints in the granite can be seen in the main face below the summit of the hill, and it was these which enabled the quarrymen to extract large rectangular blocks. The remaining half of some vertical blast holes are visible on the face. These were hand-bored and packed with gunpowder, which had just sufficient force to dislodge large blocks without shattering the rock. Such masses were then cleaved by first boring a line of small 8 cm deep holes. A pair of 'feathers' (thin half-round iron or steel plates) were placed in each hole with a steel 'plug' inserted between them, and it did not take much with a heavy hammer to split the rock fairly evenly. This 'plug and feather' method is still in use at quarries today, except that compressed air drills have replaced the old hand-borers.

Many of the surface boulders – *'moorstones'* – lying about the moors bear the marks of stone-cutting. Before about 1800, granite was split by inserting wedges in grooves chiselled in the rock, but examples of this 'wedge and groove' method are not common and most moorstones bear the holes of the 'plug and feather' type. Occasionally, there are unfinished shapes left abandoned. The best place to see these is on the west slope of Stowe's Hill, below a small quarry, to which the course of a tramway can be followed. A collection here resembles the course-stones for a **lighthouse** (9). Nearby, two parallel grooves sunk into the slope enabled cart or waggon wheels to be backed in to aid the loading of the stones.

Outside the south-west corner of Cheesewring Quarry is the curious ***Daniel Gumb's Cave*** (10). In the mid-eighteenth century, long before there was a quarry, Daniel Gumb (died 1776) built a home for himself and a 'numerous' family among the natural rocks, free of rent or rates and in a situation well suited to his occupation as stone-cutter and thinker, which earned him the name of the 'Mountain Philosopher'. The original 'cave' was beneath a 10 m-long granite slab. There were several rooms and the whole was surrounded by an enclosure. What is seen today is a reconstruction, rescued when the quarry was extended in the 1870s. The roof is a portion of the original, and bears a carving of one of Euclid's problems. It is said that Gumb was accustomed to sitting on this rock when star-gazing at night. Close-by is a portion of a doorpost carved 'D. Gumb 1735' (perhaps one of his marriage dates).

Daniel Gumb's cave.

The Cheesewring

The famous **Cheesewring** (11) also stands close to the quarry edge. This fungoid-shaped formation is about 7 m high and extremely difficult to climb without assistance as it overhangs all round. A 'support' placed to protect the Cheesewring during quarry blasting in 1869 does not in fact touch the rock. The name probably derives from its resemblance to the 'cheeses' of apple pulp built up on the press during cider making. While the Cheesewring is an extreme case, such granite tors are natural formations and are common on Bodmin Moor and Dartmoor. Simply, in times past the granite was decomposed by weathering below the surface, aided by closely jointed or shattered rock. Subsequent removal of this material downslope by 'solifluction' during the Ice Age left the resistant unweathered parts where the joints are more widely spaced. The scattered moorstones around the hillslopes are remnants of these tors.

Stowe's Hill (12) is 381 m (1,250 ft) above sea level. The horizontal joints are prominent in the three weathered tors on the summit, just behind the Cheesewring. They have splendid shapes and also feature naturally weathered basins on their top surfaces. The western rock has the 'Devil's Armchair' which offers a comfortable reclination for those wishing to tempt fate – whoever sits here becomes a poet or goes mad! Among these rocks is a half-finished stone for an apple crusher or cider press. Careful investigators will find marks of 'wedge and

Stowe's Hill, before quarrying commenced in the nineteenth century.

groove' cutting here, although the clearest examples are around the base of the Cheesewring. Some may well be the work of Daniel Gumb.

Encircling the main summit rocks are neatly cut 'fleur-de-lis' marks. These, with earlier crosses within circles, were carved to mark the limits of quarrying in the nineteenth century. One often comes across them by chance, but examples can be seen right on the quarry edge near the Cheesewring.

The main summit is surrounded by the tumbled stone wall known as **Stowe's Pound** (13), which may be of Neolithic date. The main citadel is complemented by a larger but less well defended enclosure along the hilltop to the north. Within this, it is possible to recognise circular areas where stones have been cleared for huts. Halfway along, on the west side, a 'droveway' leads down the slope from an entrance. It is worth a walk along this level hilltop settlement to the north end, both for its situation overlooking the Witheybrook Marsh and to see the ancient field system beneath the present fields of Sharptor.

The **views** from the summit of Stowe's Hill are truly magnificent. Below, to the east, stretches a patchwork of fields of east Cornwall and west Devon, backed by the mass of Dartmoor which rises at its left (north) end to 621 m at High Willhays, 23 miles (37 km) distant.

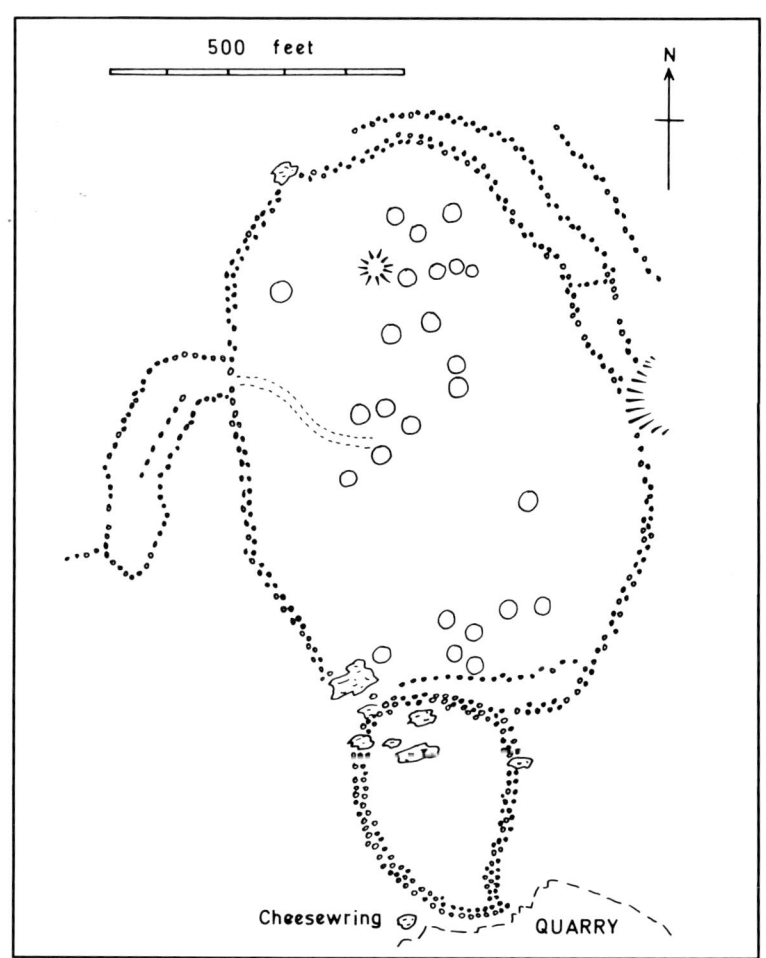

PLAN OF STOWE'S POUND

Further left, the foothills of Exmoor (c.47 miles/75 km) can be seen on a clear day. In the middle distance, the round dome of Kit Hill with its summit stack is usually prominent (7½ miles/12 km), while to the right, Plymouth (18 miles/29 km) and part of the south Devon coast are visible before Caradon Hill blocks the view. To the right of Caradon Hill, the sea and south Cornish coast include the Eddystone

Lighthouse (25 miles/40 km) and the prominent Dodman Point (26 miles/42 km). Beyond, the Lizard peninsula is visible on a clear day, with the shapes of the Goonhilly satellite tracking station (46 miles/74 km). Westwards is the distinctive horizon of the 'Cornish Alps' – the clay producing district of the Hensbarrow or St Austell Moors (18 miles/29 km). In the immediate foreground is Gold Diggings Quarry, across the head of the Witheybrook Marsh (see walk 2). To the north west is Brown Willy (8 miles/13 km), Cornwall's 'mountain' and highest point at 420 m. To the north, behind Langstone Downs and Sharp Tor, lies the long ragged ridge of Kilmar Tor (walk 4).

Summit Rocks, Stowe's Hill.

It is best to return to Minions by following the quarry track, formerly the railway. At the quarry entrance are the remains of **quarrymen's cottages** (14), built in 1864. There are crude Pythagoran diagrams carved on a rock near their south end. Next to the track, the fenced **Stowe's Shaft** (15) is 220 m deep. From here, the course of an inclined tramway can be seen descending to the site of extensive mine dressing floors below. This was the **Phoenix United Mine** (16), once the largest tin producer in east Cornwall, with workings running beneath the moor for a mile (1.6 km) to the west. Over 16,000 tons of tin and 83,000 tons of copper were produced during the mine's lifetime (1842–98). Today little remains at the surface, where there was once a mass of engine houses, shafts and ore dressing floors, and where nearly 600 persons, male and female, were employed at the height of production. Apart from a few ruins, only the large 'Account House' survives as a private dwelling. To the right, the prominent engine house and associated buildings date from an unsuccessful attempt to re-open the mine in 1907–14 by sinking the new Prince of Wales Shaft (1,193ft/364 m deep). The engine house, with its distinct square-based and brick-topped chimney stack, contained a large

80-in pumping engine, one of the last to be built for a Cornish mine. The massive granite bedstones with bolt holes for securing the cylinder can be seen inside the building. Next door is the boiler house, while a range of other buildings contained the steam winding engine and compressors. The large building behind was for engines and their boilers for working 'stamps' for crushing the tin ore. The concrete stamps 'loadings' stand outside the building. The main dressing floors were planned below these. The mine is well worth a visit, but is best reached down the road (a former railway siding) from Minions.

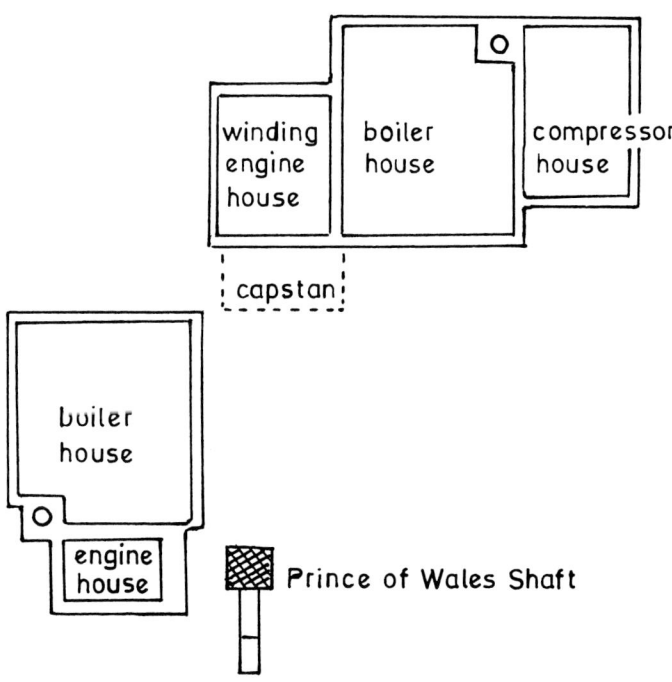

Layout of buildings at Prince of Wales Shaft, Phoenix United Mine.

At least one good Bronze Age **hut-circle** (17) can be seen just below the track where it is joined by the original quarry branch. Traces of field boundaries here are only really visible when not covered with bracken.

The track curves right and then leads straight to Minions. On the left is passed a concrete platform belonging to extensive **tin dressing floors** found on both sides of the track. This was part of **South Phoenix Mine** (18), worked intermittently until 1906-8, with a last attempt in 1920. Although Minions is in sight, turn right past grassed-over foundations (including round 'buddles') to the fenced concrete collar of the inclined Parson's Shaft, sunk on the Grace Dieu Lode in 1872. There are traces of a stamps engine house and a cobbled floor nearby; a large reservoir behind supplied water for the mine. The course of the Greenhill Lode is a short distance north, and beside the fenced North Shaft is a **whim round** with a centre stone. A horse walked in this circle to work the winding gear. Returning towards Minions, the Minions Heritage Centre is in the prominent engine house at **Houseman's Shaft.** As seen by the upper windows and chimneys, it was converted into offices and a dwelling after the pumping engine was removed. This building still dominates the back of Minions and is a feature of the skyline when seen from the western edge of Dartmoor. Immediately behind Minions is Prosper Shaft, where there are winding gear and other concrete foundations from the 1906-8 working. Just to the east is the overgrown platform and ruin of the railway's Rillaton depot. The track follows the route of the original railway into Minions.

The Cheesewring and Stowe's Hill.

The 80-in pumping engine house at Prince of Wales Shaft, Phoenix United Mine.

THE HURLERS

Situated close to Minions village, the Hurlers make an interesting excursion on their own; they can be taken in as the starting or finishing point of all walks.

The Hurlers.

The Hurlers and South Phoenix Mine.

Picnic Time on the Cheesewring. Photo: S. Bramble.

Prince of Wales Shaft, Phoenix United Mine.

THE WALK ACROSS CRADDOCK MOOR.

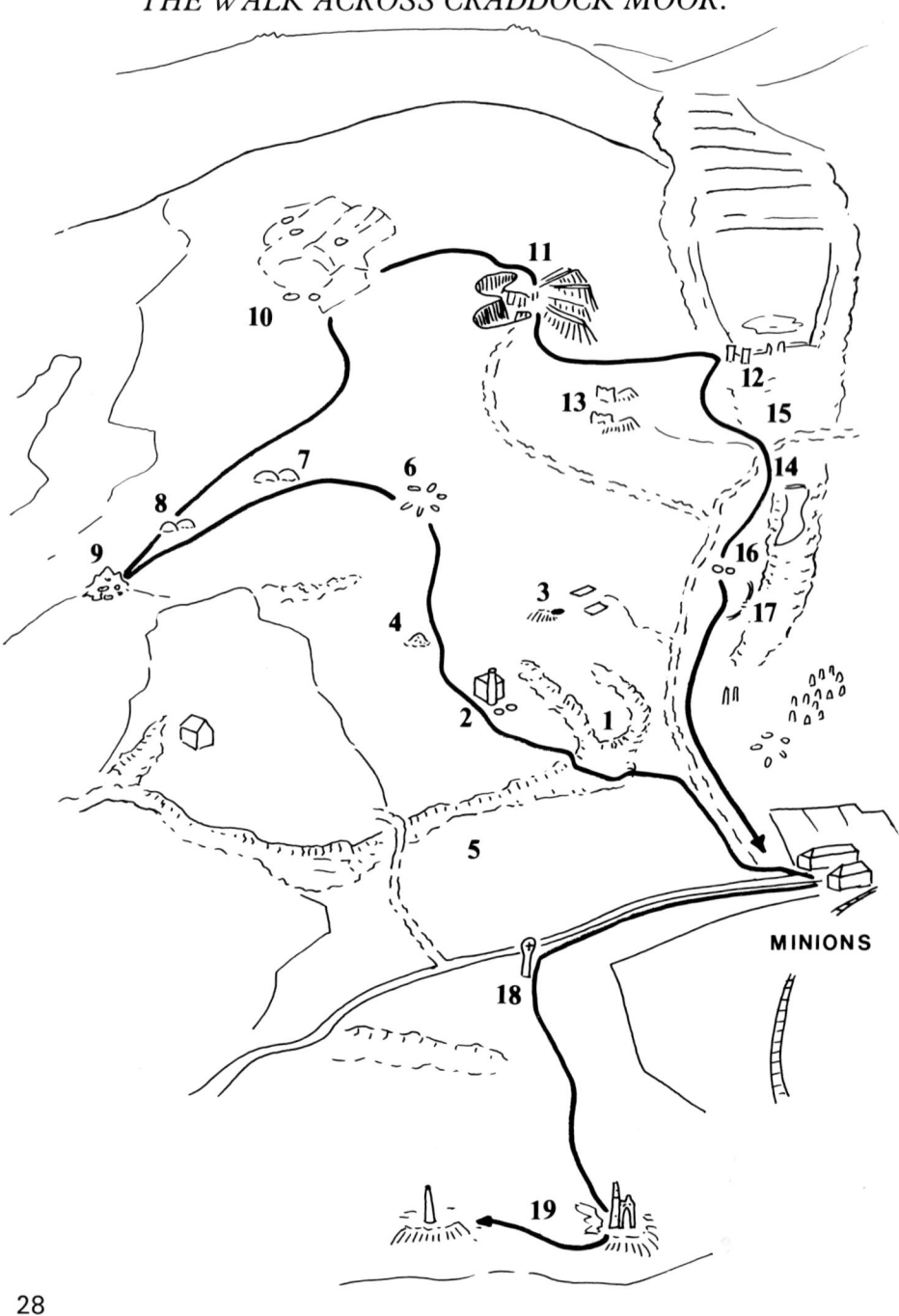

2. CRADDOCK MOOR
(Minimum 3¾ miles or 6 km)

MUCH of this route could be used as a westward extension of Cheesewring Moor. Start as for Cheesewring Moor, from the west end of Minions, but follow the track past the car park and Hurlers stone circles. Then leave the track and head away to the left, towards a ruined engine house. Deep gullies are crossed which mark the site of **tin streaming and shallow mine workings,** active from time to time until the 1930s (1). The main feature is the ruined engine house at **Silver Valley** (2), with traces of a boiler house on the west side. A steam engine worked tin stamps and dressing machinery, including three round buddles for separating the crushed tin ore. Little is known of this site, also known as New Phoenix, but 400 m north are spoil tips, foundations and a capped shaft dating from a tin working by the Canadians during World War II (3).

The moor to the north west of Silver Valley abounds in archaeology. Nearby, a large **cairn** (4), much robbed of its stone, is an Early Bronze Age burial mound. This provides a good viewpoint. It is sometimes possible to identify traces of medieval cultivation ridges – seen as faint parallel lines – on the far slopes of the small valley to the south (5).

From the cairn a delightful walk can be made across the open moor to Tregarrick Tor. Instead of the direct route, aim for the crest of the moor to locate the fallen **Craddock Moor stone circle** (6). This lies 700 m NNW of the cairn. Fifteen fallen stones remain of this circle, which has a diameter of 38 m. It is difficult to find, and it may be easier to approach it later on the route, after visiting Gold Diggings Quarry (see below). From here, follow the crest of the moor to take in two pairs of **barrows** known as 'platform cairns'. Although low, their interest lies in their carefully chosen sites. The first (7) includes a bell-shaped turf-covered cairn 14 m in diameter and about 1.5 m high. The west barrow has an outer lip with traces of an external stone kerb. The second pair of barrows (8) lies closer to the tor. Both are small mounds with robbed centres. In summer, a rich growth of bracken distinguishes them from the rest of the moorland vegetation

29

of coarse grasses and low clumps of gorse. ***Tregarrick Tor*** (9) is typical of many of the smaller granite tors on Bodmin Moor. It is at the end of a spur and overlooks the Siblyback Reservoir.

A return to the first pair of barrows and a descent north into the wide valley below is rewarded by the exploration of a ***Bronze Age farming settlement*** on the far slopes (10). Several hut-circles can be located, associated with the low walls of irregular fields. Gorse makes some difficult to find. Less obvious monuments are a small stone row and embanked avenue.

Climb east to the summit, to look down into ***Gold Diggings Quarry*** (11), which was worked by the Liskeard firm of Joseph Sweet & Sons until the 1930s. The main quarry is flooded to a depth of 18 m. Granite was sawn and dressed in sheds here, although much stone was sent by road to the firm's Liskeard works. The waste tips give an idea of how the much larger ones at Cheesewring Quarry once looked. Gold Diggings is a popular picnic place and provides a good view towards the Cheesewring and Stowe's Hill.

It is easy to return to Minions by following the quarry road. However, there are other points of interest. A short distance from the quarry, there is the low mound of a barrow just to the right (west) of the track. The fallen stones of the Craddock Moor Circle are best located from here by walking about 200 m in a line towards Tregarrick Tor.

A forest of granite posts once stood at the old dressing sheds at Gold Diggings Quarry.

Below the quarry is the head of Witheybrook Marsh. Tin works straddle the enclosed fields of the former Wardbrook Farm, demolished in 1973. There are two interesting **boundary stones** at the south west corner of the field wall (12). There was extensive mining here. Rubble is all that is left of two engine houses at **West**

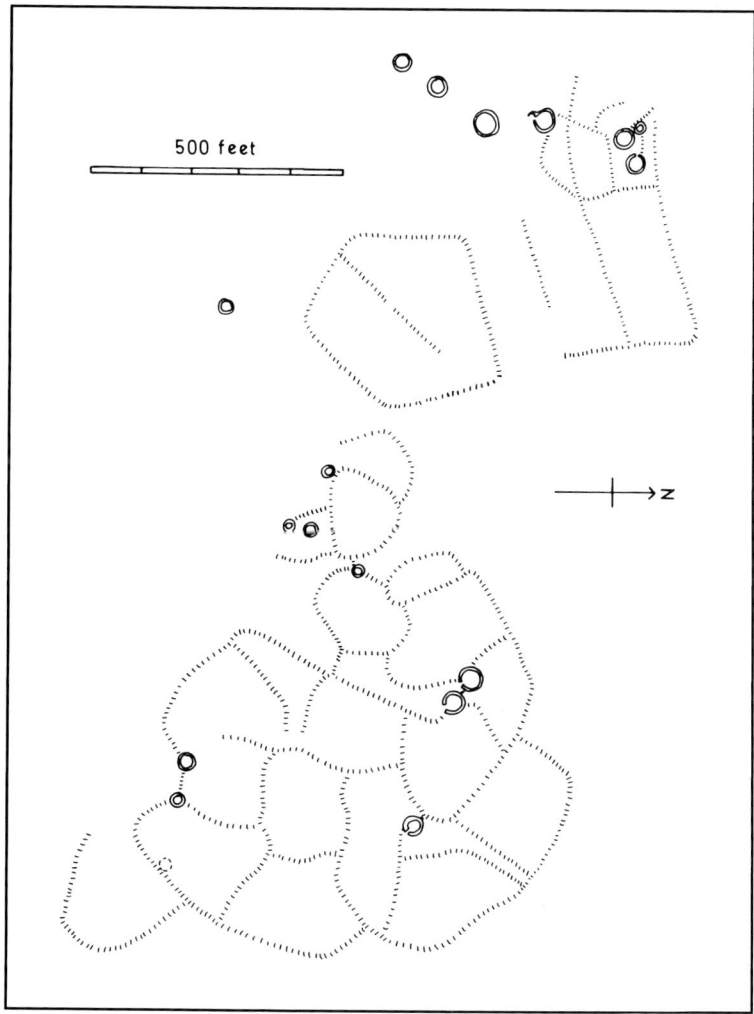

A plan of Bronze Age hut-circles and fields on Craddock Moor.

Phoenix Mine (13) on the lower slopes, and a dry leat can be followed around to the deep pond in the great tin gully (14). This supplied water for the mine engines. Below the dam, there are traces of workings and shafts of the ***Witheybrook Mine*** (15). The great gully of the Witheybrook tin works must have been worked over many years. Now flooded and overgrown, there are many interesting plants here, including sundews. Further remains can be found by keeping above the gully. A rectangular structure beside the track to Minions was a reservoir to supply water for two ***round buddles*** (16) which are well preserved nearby. The curved bank of an older ***reservoir*** to supply water for tin streaming can be seen just above the edge of the gully (17). Return to Minions along the track.

Another part of Craddock Moor lies to the south of the St Cleer road. Beside the road, half a mile (0.8 km) from Minions, is the ***Minions Cross*** (16), also known as 'Long Tom' or the 'Longstone'. This fine 3-m tall granite cross could date from the eighth or ninth centuries AD but is probably later. Its position in alignment with the Hurlers suggests that it may have been an earlier prehistoric standing stone. Strike out onto the moor to the south, to find the ruined engine house of ***Craddock Moor Mine*** (17). The engine pool still holds water. There is a good view of South Caradon Mine (walk 3) and the lowlands of south east Cornwall. A short distance to the west are dumps and a chimney of the same mine, which produced 20,110 tons of copper ore in 1856–73.

Silver Valley engine house.

Engine houses at West Phoenix Mine, with chimney of Witheybrook Mine beyond, in 1938. Photo: H. G. Ordish.

Long Tom, the Minions Cross.

Hut-circle on Craddock Moor.

Craddock Moor field system, with Siblyback Reservoir beyond.

CRADDOCK MOOR MINE

THE WALK ACROSS CARADON MOOR.

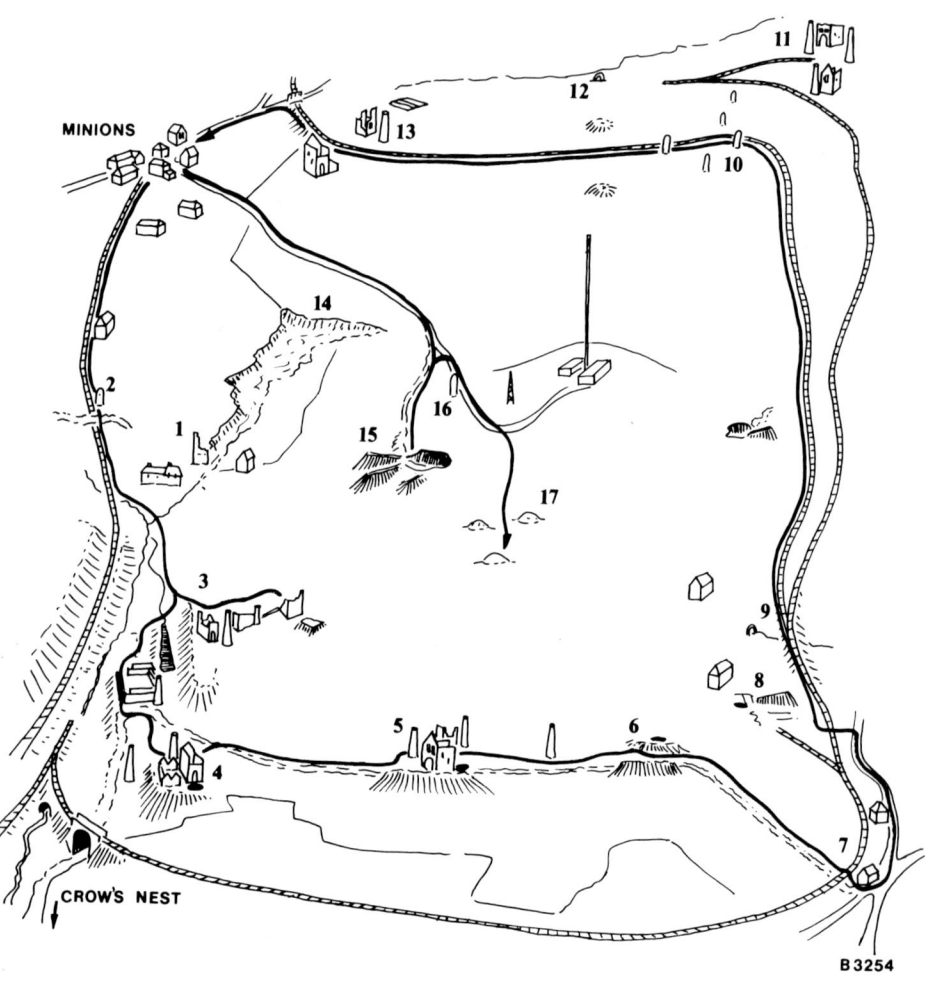

3. CARADON MOOR
(Minimum 4½ miles or 7.2 km)

LEAVE the centre of Minions, just right of the Cheesewring Hotel, to follow the early track of the Liskeard & Caradon Railway (LCR). After a small gate, there is a straight section of granite sleeper blocks between dry stone walls. It is not difficult to imagine the railway here. Pass the small sewage works to the site of **Gonamena Mine** at the top of an incline. There is little to see of the mine, although the stark corner of an engine house survives over towards Caradon Hill (1).

All trace has gone of the winding gear at the top of the **Gonamena incline,** which descends through a shallow cutting. Note the **boundary stone** marked 'LCR' on the left (2). Cross the track which now blocks the incline halfway down and continue down the old sleeper blocks until a stile gives access to the valley bottom on the left. Cross the Seaton stream to reach the extensive remains of **South Caradon Mine** (3). It was here in the Seaton gully that rich copper was discovered in 1836, which gave rise to the mining boom in the district. The mine soon became the largest and richest in Cornwall, east of St Day. When it closed in 1885, it had reached a depth of 457 m below adit and produced over 200,000 tons of copper ore. At its busiest, over 650 persons were employed above and below ground. Today, the gully is a mass of ruins and waste tips, but a description of 1863 brings the scene to life once more:

'From the top of the western slope of Caradon Hill, an excellent bird's eye view offers itself to the observer: immediately below all the mine works and buildings are clearly seen, most of them in the narrow gully . . .where every available space is occupied by railways, ore floors, engines, stamps, and the many appliances for the economical conduction of mining enterprises. Immense masses of granite debris or 'Deads' intrude themselves everywhere.'

To explore the remains it is best to strike up left onto the slopes of Caradon Hill, and work downwards. The upper ruined engine house at Pearce's Shaft is notable for its twin buttresses. This housed a 50-in pumping engine, dating from 1870. Just behind is the pool for supplying water for the engine. Surface water was precious, and a

Ruined engine house at Sump Shaft, South Caradon Mine with West Caradon across the valley.

series of leats connected to engine pools can be found in many places. While here, one can climb 250 m NNE to a small waste tip and horse whim round at Webb's Shaft. Below Pearce's Shaft are the remains of a winding engine house and pumping engine house at Sump Shaft. Just to the south of these is the 'capstan round', used for handling heavy pitwork in the shaft. There is also a magazine built into the back of a shallow excavation. The waste tips here are large and provide a good viewpoint. Across the valley, the immense tips of West Caradon Mine have been much disturbed by quarrying for roadstone. There are few remains of this rich mine, which produced 83,616 tons of copper ore in 1845–74, but the distinctive Account House survives as a farmhouse.

Below the tips of Sump Shaft, a leat still supplies water to a long reservoir, which has traces of sluices. Immediately below is the site of a waterwheel which once hauled ores from Sump Shaft. At the far end of the reservoir, two sides of a walled yard are formed by two drying and changing houses, one with a chimney, said in 1864 to have been 'most admirably adapted to meet the comforts and requirements of the men.' A third side was divided into small rooms for storing tools. The one on the far left was the barber's shop. In the valley bottom are the old cobbled floors where the copper ore was dressed by hand.

The lower end of the site is crossed by a large embankment and arch of the LCR, built in 1861 to take the line around to Tokenbury Corner and later to obviate the incline by a loop around Caradon Hill. ***The track through the arch leads to Crow's Nest, a useful access point for this part of the mine.*** There are other ruins here, but the most interesting is the engine house at ***Jope's Shaft*** (4). The boiler house walls and chimney are particularly well preserved, while inside the engine house are the cylinder bed stones.

South Caradon's long run of workings eastwards gives the appearance of three separate mines. From Jope's Shaft, gain a track (old tramway) to the remains of two pumping engine houses at ***Rule's North and South Shafts*** (5). There are also the loadings for the drums of a winding engine here. One tramway track continues through an arch beneath the waste tips to reach the site of ***Kittow's Shaft*** at the eastern limit of the mine (6). There were in fact three shafts sunk from the same point, but there is little to see today.

From here, an obvious track leads to the main road at ***Tokenbury Corner*** (7). ***This is another access point for Caradon Hill.*** The

Rule's Shaft, South Caradon Mine.

LCR crossed here and there was a siding and depot to serve nearby Pensilva village. Follow the road (B3254) north for 400 m until a gate leads left to **East Caradon Mine,** where there are waste tips, shafts and traces of buildings and dressing floors (8). The mine enjoyed brief prosperity in 1860-85, when 54,047 tons of copper ore were produced. The LCR can now be regained and followed with ease to Minions. This is the loop opened in 1877 to replace the incline. Soon, it crosses an embankment (9), where a branch on the right descends to Marke Valley Mine (see below); on the left, note the entrance to an **adit** (drainage level). Further on, there is a small overgrown granite quarry above the track, worked by J. Sweet & Sons in the 1940s.

When the track curves left around the hill, look out for at least two **granite mileposts** – '15¾' and '16' – giving the distance from Looe Quay. Also on either side of the track are four tall posts marked 'MV' to show the western boundary of the **Marke Valley Mine** sett (10). The mine was first worked unsuccessfully for tin in 1828, and then for copper in 1837-90, when 130,000 tons of ore were produced. The two remaining engine houses can be seen below (11). The lower house,

Milepost '15¾' on Caradon Hill.

Liskeard and Caradon Railway stone at Gonamena incline.

with a distinctive yawning arch of granite blocks, was erected in 1855 for a 70-in pumping engine at **Salisbury Shaft.** The upper building was for a winding engine.

Waste tips above and below the track indicate shafts of **West Rosedown Mine,** which has a stone arched adit portal deep in the valley bottom (12). At the end of a long stretch, the track curves right between two engine houses of **Wheal Jenkin,** worked for tin by the Marke Valley Mine until 1890 (13). The largest, well built house, was for a pumping engine on Bellingham's Shaft and bears the inscription 'MV 1886', the only one in the district to bear a date. The smaller engine house was for driving stamps for crushing tin ore, and traces of dressing floors and round buddles can be seen on the slopes below.

Cross the high embankment to reach the Upton Cross road at a demolished bridge. Turn left to Minions.

Rather than a circuit, a less strenuous walk is from Minions to the summit of **Caradon Hill** and back (minimum 2 miles or 3.2 km). The road to the television station gives easy access and leaves Minions to the left of the Cheesewring Hotel. As it starts to climb, note the head

Stamps engine at work, Wheal Jenkin.

Pumping engine house at Salisbury Shaft, Marke Valley Mine.

Rule's Shaft, South Caradon Mine.

of the ***Gonamena tin works*** on the right (14). This ancient working forms a huge overgrown scar, leading down to the Seaton valley.

At the cattle grid, make a detour right to ***Caradon Quarry*** (15), once worked by Joseph Sweet & Sons. Until the 1960s, there were dressing sheds, power plant and three timber derricks here. All have been cleared, but a compressed air winch lies in the flooded quarry. Return to the road and continue uphill, passing a ***boundary stone*** of East Caradon Mine – marked 'EC' – by the wall on the right (16). On the summit is a scattered cemetery of at least fifteen Bronze Age ***burial cairns.*** Those to the south are the best preserved (17), the ones near the television and radio masts having been disturbed.

Caradon Hill is a distinctive whale-backed final bastion at the south east corner of Bodmin Moor, and at 369 m (1,213 ft) gives a rewarding all-round view. One seems to look down onto Plymouth and the south coasts of Devon and Cornwall. To the north, is a fine panorama of Bodmin Moor. Sunset is a recommended time to experience the hilltop. Return to Minions by the road.

GONAMENA

THE WALK ACROSS KILMAR MOOR.

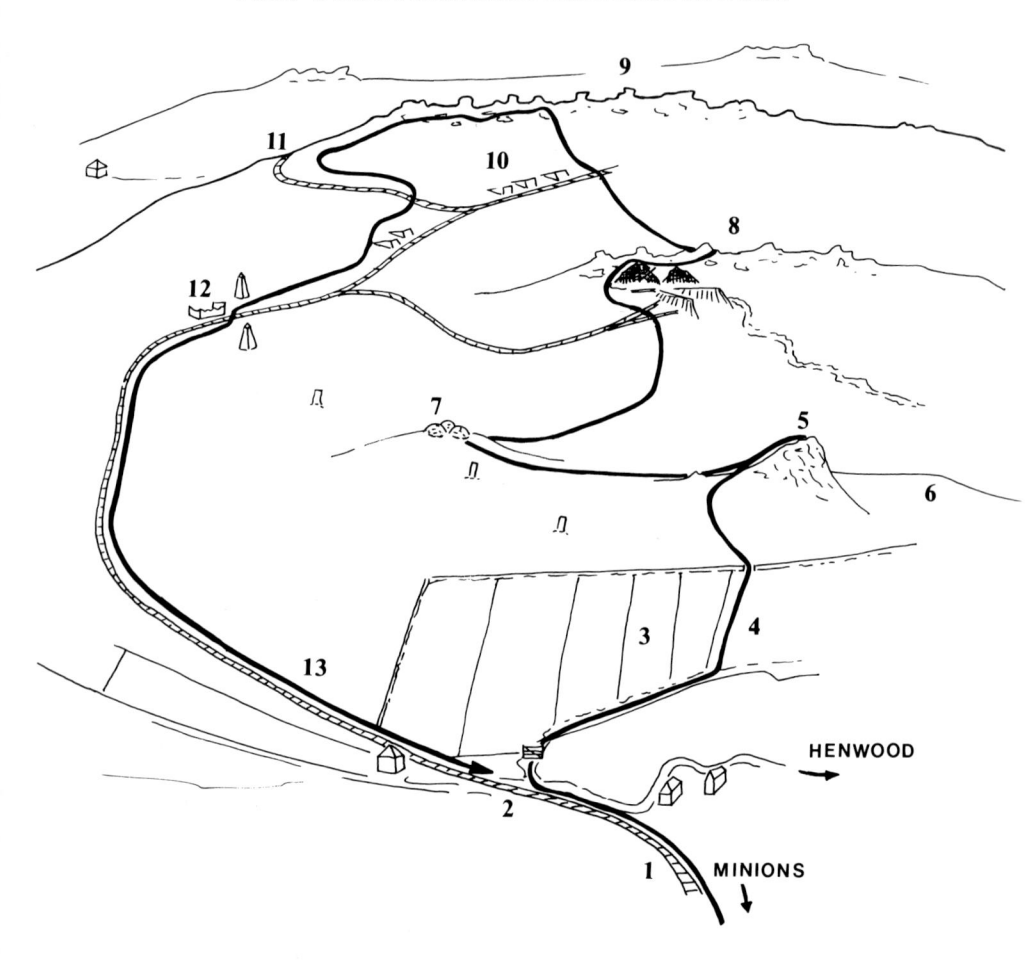

4. KILMAR MOOR
(Minimum 6½ miles or 10.4 km from Minions;
3½ miles or 5.6 km from Sharptor)

FROM Minions, take the Henwood road and by the climbing hut (formerly a water tank and then the Working Men's Institute) turn left onto the old track of the Liskeard & Caradon Railway. This soon becomes the **Kilmar Railway** (1), built in 1858 to serve the granite workings at Kilmar Tor. On the right is a good view of the Phoenix United Mine (see walk 1). There are at least five granite posts standing at ¼-mile intervals beside the track as it follows the contour of the hill. There are also some good sections of granite sleeper blocks, but note where they were poorly replaced by contractors where the line passes below the disturbed tips of Cheesewring Quarry. The old railway reaches the deep gap between Stowe's Hill and Sharp Tor, where it meets a lane to **North Wardbrook Farm** (2). *It is possible to drive to this point (Sharptor), thus avoiding the first section – follow the road towards Henwood and turn back left to Sharptor, just before entering the village.*

Cross the grassy lane and enter a gate to follow a track below large stone-walled fields on the south slopes of Langstone Downs and Sharp Tor. The banks of ploughed-out **Bronze Age fields** can be seen crossing diagonally beneath these nineteenth-century fields (3). There are **hut-circles and enclosures** within the first abandoned and unimproved field (4). Climb up here to the wall at the top where a small gate gives access to the open moor.

The craggy **Sharp Tor** (5) must now be climbed. The easiest ascent from the west (left) is unexpectedly narrow and well worth the scramble. At 378 m (1,240 ft), this is a good viewpoint, particularly towards Kilmar Tor. Lundy Island (45 miles/72 km) is also visible on a clear day. There are **prehistoric field boundaries** on the moor immediately below to the east (6), best explored in winter or spring when not covered with bracken.

From here, turn back to climb the easy slope to the open summit of Langstone Downs. There is no tor here, but three large **ruinous cairns** (7). These are in line with four **granite posts** marked 'BSK

Traces of prehistoric field systems beneath nineteenth century enclosures at Sharp Tor.

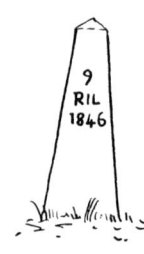

1-4' to indicate the bounds of the Kilmar granite sett of 1865. These can be followed north west to the ruined blacksmith's shop (see below), but a detour to the long ridge of **Bearah Tor** is more rewarding for its curiously poised rocks with basins (8). There are small granite **quarries** on the south side, with waste tips and remains of old timber derrick cranes. A branch of the Kilmar Railway reaches the quarry from over the moor to the west.

Bearah is overshadowed by the greater **Kilmar Tor,** across the high plateau of Twelve Men's Moor to the north (9). This is a fantastic ridge of granite tors, with the third highest summit in Cornwall (396 m or 1,299 ft). Among the rocks is a conspicuous leaning 'Cheesewring' towards the west end. The scattered moorstones on the gentle southern slopes beneath the tor were worked by quarrymen in the mid-nineteenth century. In 1868, there were 80 men and boys at work, with 60 more at Bearah. This was the destination of the Kilmar Railway, where cut granite was loaded onto trucks by means of solid **ramps** beside the track (10). As well as the branch to Bearah, a later one of 1879 around to a small *quarry* on the north side of Kilmar (11). The granite sleeper blocks are followed with ease. As at Stowe's Hill, the summit rocks of Kilmar and Bearah were protected from quarrying by a series of carved 'fleur-de-lis' symbols.

Kilmar Tor is a lofty, and often windy, viewpoint, with the north Cornish coast and Lundy Island visible on a clear day. Immediately north of the tor are the lower ridges of Trewortha Tor (left), with a coffin-shaped rock basin known as 'King Arthur's Bed' at the west end, and Hawk's Tor (right). Both are worthy of a visit, as are hut-circles on the level moor between and a small cairn circle with cist at the foot of the steep north slope of Kilmar. However, these are beyond the range of this described walk.

The Kilmar Railway can be followed back to Sharptor and Minions. Just before the line curves left into a shallow cutting, the ruins of a *blacksmith's shop* are seen on the right (12). This served the granite cutters at Kilmar, sharpening and mending tools. Two Rillaton *boundary stones* marked 'RIL 1846, 9 & 10' are close by (see walk 1). The small stream here is known as Kilmar Lake, and just below the ruin it was tapped by the **Phoenix Leat,** which carried water to the engines and dressing floors on Phoenix United Mine, 2¼ miles (3.6 km) away.

As the railway descends, the now dry Phoenix Leat emerges on the right to run along at the back of some fields just below. From this point, **Bronze Age hut-circles and field systems** are visible on the slopes of Langstone Downs above (13). This is also a good place to view the Witheybrook Marsh. Looking down the valley to the north, one can see the earthworks of a projected railway extension to Trewint, Camelford and Launceston, dating from 1884.

The track passes behind North Wardbrook Farm to reach Sharptor. The circuit is complete. If returning to Minions, a walk below the west side of Stowe's Hill may be preferred if the railway track was followed on the outward journey.

Fleur-de-lis carvings are found at Cheesewring, Bearah and Kilmar.

The three cairns atop Langstone Downs.

Bearah Tor Quarry.

Sharptor from Phoenix United Mine. Photo: S. Bramble.

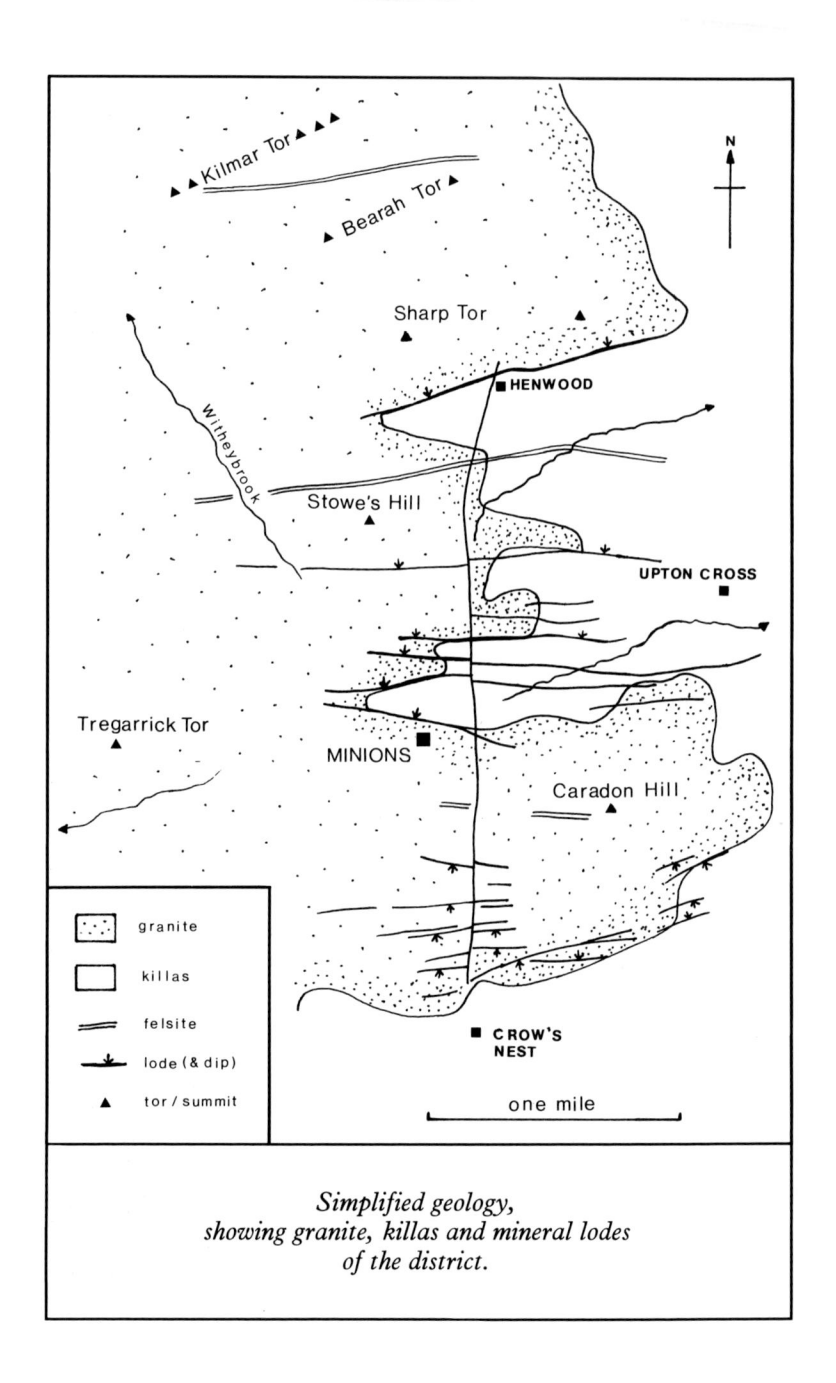

*Simplified geology,
showing granite, killas and mineral lodes
of the district.*

GEOLOGY

THIS is solid country. Most of the rock in the area is granite which was intruded as magma beneath rocks of a high mountain chain during the Variscan orogeny about 280 million years ago. Weathering and erosion in the intervening years has revealed the granite at the surface down the spine of South West England, from Dartmoor to the Isles of Scilly. Bodmin Moor is the second largest of these upstanding bosses, which are all connected at depth.

The granite is 'silver-grey' in colour to use a quarrymen's term. It consists mainly of crystals of glassy grey or white quartz, white feldspar and shiny mica (black biotite and white muscovite). Black needle-like crystals of tourmaline are present in small quantities; they form schorl faces on the sides of joints exposed at Cheesewring Quarry. The nature of the granite can be seen, for example, in the clean faces and among the rubble at this quarry. Horizontal and vertical joints, which formed as the granite cooled, are also displayed in the faces.

The steep moorland edge coincides with the contact of the granite with country rocks known as killas, the name given to the highly baked Devonian-age slates and clays of the 'metamorphic aureole' which surrounds the granite. The variety of its colour can be seen on the old mine waste dumps. For example, at Phoenix United Mine it is mainly pink, buff and light grey in colour, while elsewhere it is a brick red or pale brown; at Wheal Jenkin a distinctive blue is present.

Felsite, or elvan, is a fine-grained granite which was injected as wall-like dykes into long cracks developed in the granite and killas, probably before the lower part of the granite solidified. A long elvan dyke crosses Stowe's Hill and continues east into the killas. Some of the stones of Stowe's Pound are of this finer grained rock.

At this south-east corner of Bodmin Moor, the granite-killas contact is intersected by parallel tin and copper lodes, generally trending east-west, and upon which the nineteenth-century mining industry was based. These mineral lodes were formed during the late-stage cooling of the granite, when fissures were infilled with ores deposited from rising hot gases and solutions. They vary between 0.5

m and 4.5 m wide; the Phoenix lodes to the north of Minions dip to the south at 70°, while the Caradon lodes dip north. Both are cut by a north-south cross-course or fault. The Phoenix Main Lode contains earthy iron ore, native copper, black copper ore, malachite, vitreous copper, copper pyrites, iron pyrites and cassiterite (tin ore) to the very bottom of the mine. Many of these minerals can be found on the spoil tips on the site of the mine, while wolfram (tungsten) and zinc blende have also been found in the district. Cheesewring Quarry has been noted for rare minerals. Bertrandite and phenacite were previously unknown in Britain until recorded here in 1904-5; less scarce are anatase, chlorite, purple fluorite and wolframite.

LANDFORMS AND LANDSCAPE

THE vertical and horizontal joints which formed as the granite cooled have had a great influence on the landforms of the moor, of which the summit tors are the most dramatic features. The tors and quarry faces all show the joints to good effect. At Cheesewring, it will be noted how the horizontal joints (or 'pseudo-bedding planes') conform to the shape of the hill. Indeed, seen from the south, they wrap around the summit like the rings of an onion, forming a dome and dipping to the east and west.

The sides of the upstanding tors are defined by the vertical joints which tend to be at right angles to each other, while the horizontal joints give the granite blocks between the appearance of being piled up one upon the other. Two different theories describe tor formation. One has it that during a warm humid climate weakly acid water penetrated the joints and rotted the granite to 'growan' down to the water table. This had most effect in the well jointed areas, which presented a greater surface area to this agent of chemical weathering. In contrast, a second theory believes that tor formation results from mechanical weathering during the Ice Age. Although not covered by an ice cap, periglacial areas such as Bodmin Moor were subjected to freezing to a great depth. Continuous freezing and thawing in closely spaced joints would weaken the rock beneath the surface.

Both theories, however, agree that the weathered material was removed by the same process of 'solifluction' in the Ice Age. This took place during milder seasons, when the upper surface of the permafrost

The Cheesewring.

thawed and this saturated material moved slowly downslope, carrying with it some of the partly weathered blocks. These clitters can be seen radiating from the summits, such as around Cheesewring and Stowe's Hill. The remaining tors are the more resistant blocks defined by wider-spaced jointing. Their edges have become rounded by weathering.

Some top stones have been so weathered beneath that they have become delicately poised and can be rocked with relative ease. These 'logan' stones can be found on Bearah Tor and Kilmar Tor. It was said that the topmost stone of the Cheesewring could be moved with a pole, but this is no longer so. There was also a legend that whenever it heard a cock crow (at midnight?) the stone would move around three times. The upper surfaces of some tors have curious round basins once thought by eighteenth-century antiquaries to be 'Druidical'. They are natural, formed by the initial weathering of feldspar crystals by acid water at weaker points which then opened out. See these on the very summits at Cheesewring, Bearah and Kilmar.

The leaning western rock at Kilmar Tor. (J. Allen).

The effect of jointing is visible in the wider landscape too, especially around the Witheybrook valley and Twelve Men's Moor. The course of the Witheybrook conforms to the jointing pattern as it flows north and then turns abruptly east at Trewortha Marsh. On Twelve Men's Moor and Langstone Downs, the remarkable east-west parallel ridges centred on Kilmar Tor (resistant wide-spaced joints) are separated by broad cols (closer joints), and these are matched by 'gorges' and 'basins' along the north-south Witheybrook valley. It may be that the main valleys such as the Witheybrook and the parallel south-flowing River Fowey were first etched into existing areas of deep kaolinised (rotted) granite along the principal structure lines.

Without the tors, the moorland scene is one of rounded slopes and plateau surfaces. The latter may be the remnants of ancient erosion surfaces, and 'platforms' can be recognised at a number of different levels. The highest and most obvious platform is at about 300 m on Craddock Moor, but traces elsewhere include a slight levelling on the north slope of Caradon Hill.

Clothing these moorland bones is a vegetation which has been modified by climatic changes and man's influence. With its altitude, acid soils and an annual rainfall up to 1500 mm, the upland moors have always been a marginal area for farming. Abandoned Bronze Age field systems are evidence of better conditions in the past but now only a few modern-day farms and their fields stand out like islands surrounded by the unimproved moor. Cattle, sheep and ponies graze the open moor, which has course purple moor grass and bent-fescue grasses. Gorse and heather are present, although the latter has declined due to overgrazing and 'swaling' (deliberate burning to encourage fresh shoots for grazing). Bracken is also found around the clitter-strewn slopes, while the hardy bilberry prefers the higher and more north-facing slopes.

Valley peats have been disturbed by tin streaming, but here plant species include cotton grass, marsh violet, bog asphodel, hare's tail and sundews. Willow scrub may be found here too. The upland landscape may have had some woodland in prehistoric times, but it is now virtually treeless apart from the occasional leaning and wind-stunted hawthorn. In contrast, large modern conifer plantations at Smallacoombe and Halvana dominate the scene to the west and north west from the summit of Kilmar Tor. More interesting are the fern and lichen-draped oak woods found in the deep valleys, cut where streams tumble off the granite at the steep moorland edge.

Summit tors on Stowe's Hill.

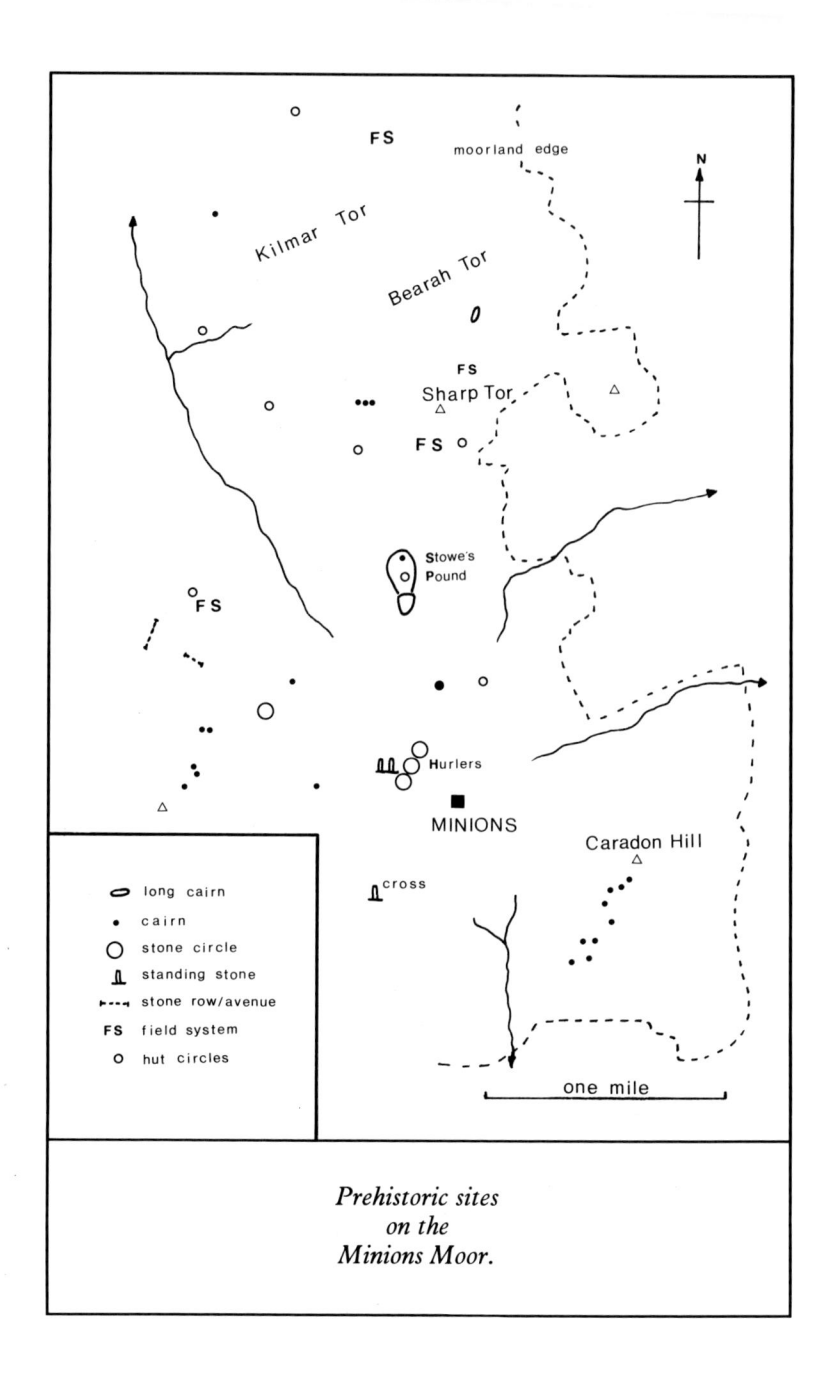

Prehistoric sites on the Minions Moor.

ARCHAEOLOGY

SCATTERED finds of flints show that man has been present on Bodmin Moor since at least Mesolithic times (c.8,000 BC onwards). The first few monuments are Neolithic, while the Early Bronze Age saw much activity with ritual monuments – burial cairns, stone circles, stone rows, standing stones – settlements and field systems. Their location hints at tin streaming too. The moor, always a marginal area for settlement and farming, seems to have been abandoned due to deteriorating climate. Thereafter, there is little evidence until medieval recolonisation in the twelfth to early fourteenth centuries, with settlements, fields and crosses. The wealth of prehistory is more than matched by the nineteenth-century industrial archaeology of this small area. April is the best time for exploring the lesser monuments, as the vegetation is then low and there is no bracken.

Already rich in prehistory, it is surprising that new sites (indeed, new types of site) have been discovered since the 1970s. This is due in part to a detailed six-year survey of Bodmin Moor made jointly by the Cornwall Archaeological Unit, the Royal Commission on the Historical Monuments of England and English Heritage.

Neolithic (c.4000-2500BC) Trethevy Quoit (SX 259688) lies just off the 'Minions Moor' area, but as the grandest chambered tomb in Cornwall it is too good to ignore. It can be reached from Crow's Nest. A long cairn with a collapsed chamber (SX 263743) was recognised as recently as 1983 beside the track leading to Bearah Tor Quarry. Stowe's Pound, the massive stone enclosure around the summit of Stowe's Hill, is now felt to be Neolithic. Similar hilltop enclosures are at Roughtor on Bodmin Moor, Helman Tor near St Austell, and an excavated site at Carn Brea near Camborne. The tumbled wall of the main defended enclosure still survives up to 5m high on one side. Among the rocks within the outer enclosure to the north there are cleared platforms ('hut stances') for round timber huts. At the far north end are the walls of a large stone hut-circle.

Early Bronze Age (c.2500–1500BC) Burial cairns are the equivalent of the earthen round barrows of southern England. Some are large, mostly on crests and hilltops, such as Caradon Hill and

57

Cairn circle and cist, north slope of Kilmar Tor.

Langstone Downs. Those on Craddock Moor include types known as 'platform cairns'. Some cairns contain a cist – as at Kilmar (SX 245750), which is surrounded by a stone kerb circle 3.2 m in diameter. The Rillaton Barrow is the most famous on Bodmin Moor. Prominent on Rillaton Common, it appears to be aligned with the Hurlers, 500 m downslope to the SSW. It is a large barrow, perhaps 3 m high, with a deep depression in the centre. A stone cist exposed at the east end, measuring 1.8 m x 1.1 m x 0.76 m, is a reconstruction of 1901. The barrow was first opened in 1837 by workmen said to be searching for stone to build a mine engine house. John Harris witnessed 'a crowd of half-nude men digging ruthlessly into the old grave barrow.' Finding nothing in the centre, they dug a trench and discovered the cist. Inside were crumbling human bones with a pot. Apparently this was broken by the workmen and the famous gold cup was found within. There was also a metal 'rivet' and the remains of a bronze dagger blade about 25 cm long, but this was broken on removal. Having been sent to King William IV, who died soon afterwards, the Rillaton Gold Cup passed into Queen Victoria's private collection. King George V is said to have used it in his dressing room to hold his collar studs before the cup was finally presented to the British Museum in 1936. A copy is in the Royal Cornwall Museum, Truro. The Rillaton Gold Cup is 8.25 cm high; it has corrugated sides and was beaten from a single lump of

The Pipers standing stones at the Hurlers.

gold. The handle is attached by three rivets and washers, top and bottom, in a very similar fashion to a cup found at Fritzdorf in Germany. It is dated to the Early Bronze Age and such rich graves belong to the 'Wessex Culture' – most burials are in Southern England, so this one in the far west is interesting (the tin connection?).

Other ritual monuments include the famous Hurlers, signposted and now managed by Cornwall Heritage Trust. There are three circles here: North Circle 35 m diameter, 11 stones standing; Central Circle 43 m diameter, 14 stones standing (also a central stone); South Circle 33 m diameter, 2 stones standing. In the 1930s the monument was placed in the care of H.M. Office of Works and a small excavation took place before some stones were re-erected. The area within the north circle was found to be paved in granite, while between this and the central circle was a rough stone pavement 2 m wide. Some stones have evidence of hammer dressing above ground level, and this dressing may have taken place on-site because the interior of the central circle was found to be covered with crystals. An iron fence was erected around the whole site until it was removed in the early 1960s. Local tradition has it that the stones are men turned to stone for profaning the Lord's Day by playing hurling, a theme which occurs elsewhere with dancers. There are also two standing stones, 'The Pipers', about 100 m to the west. They are related in some way.

Hut-circle on Craddock Moor.

The Craddock Moor Circle is more difficult to find as all the stones have fallen. One of its 15 stones shows marks of the stone-cutter. The circle has a diameter of 38 m and was first 'discovered' in about 1923.

Also on Craddock Moor is a stone row 244 m long and aligned NE-SW (SX 239720-SX 241722). The stones are very low and are spaced about 1 m apart. Stone rows were once unique to Dartmoor, but they have now been recognised on Bodmin Moor. Another new feature is an 'embanked avenue' (SX 244721), discovered in 1984. About 55 m long, it has 'two sets of twin parallel banks' aligned NW-SE. There are traces of kerb stones. Its function is unclear but it may be associated with stone circles.

Settlements and field systems can be explored. Craddock Moor has an extensive farming settlement, with fields and hut-circles on south and west slopes. Walls of upright stones are well defined on the upper part of the site, enclosing large irregular-shaped fields which appear to have been added to in turn over the years. The low walls would have supported a fence or thorn hedge to enclose stock. A 'droveway' onto the open moor on the uphill side suggests stock were kept, but evidence that at least some of the fields were ploughed is seen where small lynchets have formed against the lower walls. At least nine hut-circles up to 9 m diameter are incorporated into the field walls.

Hut-circles have thick walls of granite moorstone which supported the rafters of a thatched conical roof. Doorways are sometimes marked by doorposts. On the lower west slope is a group of seven huts, and rather poor field boundaries but of a more rectilinear pattern. Gorse covers part of the site.

Impressive banks or lynchets lie diagonally beneath the nineteenth-century fields on the SW slope of Sharp Tor. Viewed from Stowe's Hill, the pattern of this field system shows up well in the shadow from the evening sun. Some hut-circles are in the overgrown fields below Sharp Tor, but to the west, there are huts and fields on the slopes of Langstone Downs, where they are intersected by the Kilmar Railway. On the east slope of Sharp Tor (and best viewed from its summit) are linear field boundaries. There are overgrown hut-circles below the west end of Kilmar Tor. Clearer examples, up to 13 m diameter, are beside the Trewortha Farm track on the col north of Kilmar.

Medieval period (AD 1066–1540). Later monuments include the leaning Minions Cross, also known as the 'Longstone' or 'Long Tom', beside the highest point on the Minions-St Cleer road. This splendid, though simple, cross is 3 m high. Its alignment with the Hurlers and Rillaton Barrow suggests it may be a prehistoric standing stone which has been adapted as a wayside cross. Further down the road, and outside the moor, the earlier King Doniert's Stone (c AD 875) is worth visiting.

With a keen eye, narrow parallel cultivation ridges can be detected on the moorland slope of Caradon Hill (SX 268712), Craddock Moor (SX 254708) and Hawk's Tor (SX 253759). This last can be seen from Kilmar Tor. Also within sight of Kilmar is Trewortha Marsh (SX 227761), where at least nine medieval long-houses were excavated in 1891-2 by Rev. Sabine Baring-Gould. Small enclosures may have been for stock, while it is likely that tin-streaming in the nearby Witheybrook valley supplemented the farmers' income. The site overlies earlier Bronze Age huts and cairns. One of the ruins here may have been 're-occupied' by navvies during the building of the LCR extension in the 1880s.

There is evidence that peat or turf was cut for fuel around the moor. The dried turfs were stacked on *turf steeds*, which are curious rectangular features with a trench around a low mound. They probably post-date the medieval period. There is one in line between the Hurlers car park and the central circle, and two good examples on the edge of Witheybrook Marsh (SX 247731), not far from Gold Diggings Quarry.

Old turf steed above the Witheybrook Marsh.

TIN STREAMING

BEFORE the 1830s, the principal mineral sought among these wild and remote hills was tin. The earliest operations worked the gravels containing heavier tinstones (cassiterite) eroded from mother lodes and deposited in the valley floors. The physical remains of these streamworks by the 'Old Men' are impossible to date with certainty, but the wealth of prehistoric sites in the area suggests some activity as early as the Bronze Age. Most valley floors have been turned over by tin streamers more than once as methods of recovery improved, in the medieval period (when the area came under the Stannary jurisdiction of Foweymore) and then in the nineteenth and early twentieth centuries.

Two large and ancient openworks lie to the west of Stowe's Hill and Caradon Hill. Both were already extensive by 1808. Notable is the 'Old Tin Dike' (the deep gully with a pond) above Witheybrook Marsh. It was at the head of the marsh, beneath 1.5 m of peat, that the Phoenix Mine adventurers later found old streamers' floors together with heaps of cleared tin ore ready for smelting. Downstream to the north, the bed and margins of Trewortha Marsh bear evidence of past tin streaming. Other streaming can be seen in the Trewalla valley running west from the top of the Witheybrook tinwork towards Siblyback Reservoir. On the western flank of Caradon Hill, the Gonamena tinworks is marked and named 'Tin Work' on the first edition one-inch Ordnance Survey map of 1809 (surveyed 1802-3). It covered about 4.45 ha. and had already made 'considerable and profitable returns' by 1863.

After sinking a 'hatch' or shaft to test the tin-bearing gravel, the method of working was to drive a level up from below (to take away water and waste), and remove the overburden above by hand or washing it out by a stream of water. The streamers directed a flow of water onto the exposed tin ground – already loosened by picks – which was allowed to flow through a 'tye', a sloping board which trapped the heavier tin gravels and larger stones while the lighter stuff washed away. Uneven ground is the characteristic sign of tin streaming, but sometimes parallel channels and banks of waste can be identified

Local inhabitant enjoying the pond at the Witheybrook tinworks.

where streaming has been systematic.

Along the sides of the Witheybrook gully, curved dams mark the site of now dry reservoirs where water could be stored for use in the streamworks. Some have narrow leats (water courses) leading to or from them. One of the largest (at SX 256717) has a curving dam 60 m long and a leat NE from it.

The richer tinstones were sent for smelting without further treatment. In earlier times, smelting took place in small 'blowing houses' which had water-powered bellows. The small quantities of tin produced were poured into stone moulds to form ingots. The poorer grades of ore were crushed in stamps to release the waste.

EARLY MINING

THERE is clear evidence that the Old Men also worked along the backs of the principal lodes. They left lines of shallow pits and burrows, especially seen across the open moor between Minions and Stowe's Hill (walk 1), where these follow the Jenkin, Prosper, Grace Dieu, Greenhills, Great Shelstone's (or Trelawney's) and Stowe's

(Phoenix) Lodes. 'Grace Dew' is mentioned in 1570 and they must have been active before 1727 when W. Harvey described 'the remarkable tinworks of Shilstone, Berry-work, Gracydew, Cornerwork, Chapnawell, Gadawork, with others.' When re-worked in the nineteenth century, the back of Phoenix Lode was found to have been laid open for about a mile (1.6 km), while to the south Trelawney's Lode had been worked for tin down to 36 m, but deeper workings must have been hampered by water and restricted by the lack of pumping gear.

Stowe's Mine appears to have been the first deep mine, and a Newcomen engine is said to have been erected here as early as 1730. The mine is named on Thomas Martyn's Map of Cornwall (1748), along with the Witheybrook Tin Works, as well as lode-back workings near Marke Valley. 'Stows Mine' is on the first edition one-inch Ordnance Survey map of 1809 (surveyed 1802-3). Also known as Wheal Julia, the mine became part of the Cornwall Great United Mining Association's attempts to open up the mining district in 1836-7. On 2nd September 1836, the CGUMA directors 'regaled their workmen and a party of gentlemen, with a good and substantial old English dinner, on the open moor of Caradon, to which 210 persons sat down.' Activities were concentrated at Stowe's Mine, Clanacombe Mine and Wheal Jenkin. A steam engine was erected in 1836-7 (the parts brought overland from Tideford Quay and Cotehele Quay) for stamping and pumping via flat rods at Wheal Jenkin and Wheal Prosper, 'in order to sink on that bunch of tin.' The site of this engine lies just east of the curving railway embankment at Wheal Jenkin. A map of 1838 marks an 'old engine house' here, but there is a pumping engine at Engine Shaft at Clanacombe Mine – could it be that the engine was moved and re-erected on a more promising mine? The Clanacombe site became the centre of the Phoenix Mine and a 36-in engine was recorded here in 1844, perhaps that seen in the view 'The Cheese Wring and Sharptor, Cornwall', illustrated in Allen's History of Liskeard.

The Wheal Jenkin engine house as drawn on a map of 1837.

Clanacombe and Stow's sections of Cornwall Great United Mine, 1837–8. This later became the site of the Phoenix United Mine.

THE MINING BOOM

ALTHOUGH tin had been streamed and mined in a small way for centuries, it was copper that started the mining boom that lasted 50 years or more in the district. The 1830s saw the first serious mining attempts led by the Cornwall Great United Mining Association, Marke Valley Mine and South Caradon Mine. The boom was kindled at South Caradon in 1836 when, after three years' searching, Captain James Clymo, his son Peter and the brothers Thomas and Richard Kittow struck a rich copper lode on the east side of the Seaton valley. (James Clymo was also agent, and Thomas Kittow chairman of the CGUMA). Thus the working 'adventurers' became rich overnight for an outlay of only £640, a most unusual occurrence for the discoverers to benefit in this way. The continuation of the lode across the valley into West Caradon Mine was confirmed and within a few years the Liskeard & Caradon Railway was serving the expanding mines.

Soon, all the mine properties in the district had been laid out as 'setts' and the landowners received a royalty on the value of ores sold. South Caradon's ores contained up to 11% copper, while Marke Valley's were as little as 4.4%. Because of the large quantities of coal required for smelting, it was best to ship the ores to Swansea and other smelting ports in South Wales. A convenient two-way trade developed, with the ships returning with coal for the steam engines on the mines.

In the end, the mines were becoming increasingly more expensive to work at depth and could not compete against falling copper prices brought about by cheaper ores from foreign mines (many, ironically, worked by Cornish miners who were forced to emigrate to find employment). While the Caradon copper mines failed in 1885, the tin mines to the north around Phoenix were able to continue for some years until they too succumbed to falling prices due to cheaper foreign tin. Phoenix United was in liquidation for three years before closing in 1898. Unlike copper, tin was always smelted in Cornwall.

During its lifetime, 1837-85, South Caradon Mine produced 217,820 tons of copper ore. At closure, there were 12 large engines on the sett which extended for over a mile (1.6 km). Six ruinous engine

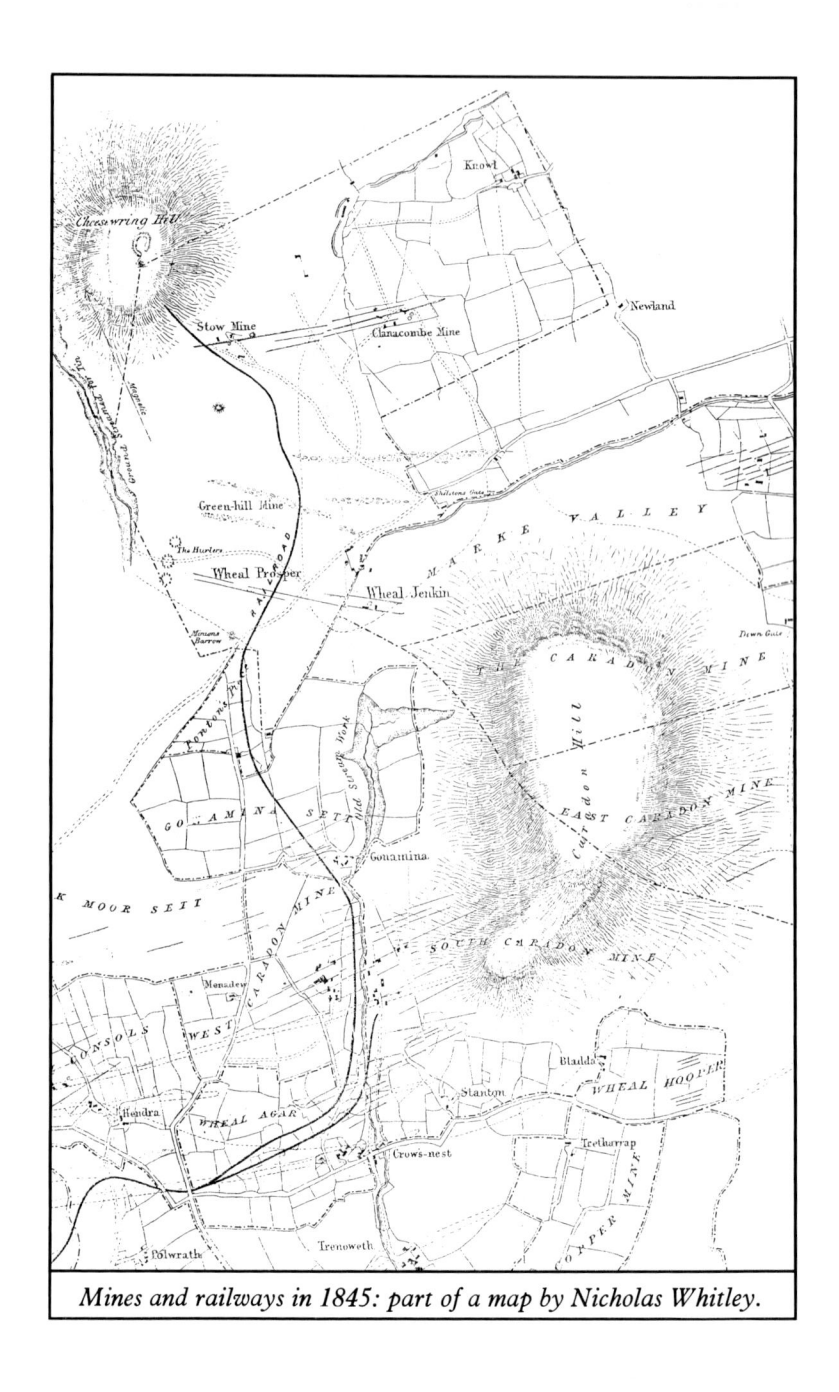

Mines and railways in 1845: part of a map by Nicholas Whitley.

houses still survive, among them an unusual house for a horizontal 22-in winding engine erected above Sump Shaft in 1844. New for the district was a 'man-engine', installed at Jope's Shaft in 1872 and worked from a whim engine which had been built eight years earlier. Access to and from deep levels by ladderways exacted a high toll on the miners' health, and man-engines went a long way to relieve this hardship. The South Caradon one was moved late in the mine's life to Kittow's Shaft on the east of the sett. Across the Seaton valley, neighbouring West Caradon Mine produced 4,128 tons of 9¼% copper ore at its height in 1851, when 553 persons (363 men, 83 women and 107 children) were employed. Today, the account house (now a dwelling) and part of the pumping engine house at Elliott's Shaft are the only significant monuments left at the surface of a mine which once had a pumping engine, two whim engines, a stamps engine, engine pools, leats, tramways, cobbled dressing floors, a changing house, smithy and carpenter's shop. Westwards along the same rich mineral tract, the ruins of an engine house and isolated chimney bear witness to the smaller and less productive Craddock Moor Mine (1856-73). The Caradon copper lodes were exploited eastwards too, where there is little trace now of East Caradon Mine (worked 1860-85 but especially rich in the first 16 years) and Glasgow Caradon Consols (1864-85). The waste tip of the latter can be seen just east of the B3254 at Caradon Farm near Tokenbury Corner.

Marke Valley Mine was north of Caradon Hill, the main site down near Upton Cross. It produced 128,737 tons of copper ore in 1845-86. The main shareholders were based in Salisbury, hence the names Sarum Lode and Salisbury Shaft. This rather overgrown site has two interesting engine houses and the course of a branch from the LCR. The sett also included West Rosedown Mine, a small working, and Wheal Jenkin, to which attention was turned during the later years in an attempt to mine tin. The fine pumping engine house here at Bellingham's Shaft is unusual for a datestone ('M.V. 1886'). The beam engine came from South Caradon Mine which had closed in the previous year. Part of the boiler house remains, but the stack fell in the 1950s. The whim engine house has gone, but downslope a smaller engine house has a stack and boiler house walls. The engine worked stamps for crushing the ore, and below are extensive dressing floors, with round buddles and tanks. 385 tons of black tin were produced in 1881-90.

Surface plan of South Caradon Mine.

Phoenix United Mine was the richest tin mine in east Cornwall, producing 16,359 tons of black tin and 83,000 tons of copper ore in the period 1842-98. Wheal Phoenix was started in 1842 in search of copper, stimulated by the success of South Caradon, and for a time it was among the county's top copper producers. As the price of copper fell, the mine was able to turn to tin which lay alongside the copper in the same lode. In 1870, the West Phoenix Mine was taken over to form Phoenix & West Phoenix United, later known as Phoenix United Mine. The two mines' dressing floors were kept separate on the main site, where there were once eight engine houses for pumping, winding and stamping. There were shafts, four more engines and an incline to the west. Now the busy site is mostly rubble, although the account house remains.

South Phoenix Mine is dominated by the tall pumping engine house at Houseman's Shaft, which was later converted to a dwelling (note the upper windows, blocked bob wall and chimneys). It is now the Minions Heritage Centre. This mine worked on many occasions for tin and copper, but never very successfully. There was a 25-in winding and stamps engine at Parson's Shaft, where there are also reservoirs and dressing floors with circular buddles and long tanks descending the slope. Parson's Shaft is distinguished by a concrete collar. It was sunk in 1872 at 39^0 on the lie of Grace Dieu Lode and, when re-opened in 1888-92, a tramroad was fitted in this shaft, with skips and tipping waggons. This was before the system was in general use in the Cornish mines further west. The vertical Houseman's Shaft intersects Parson's Shaft at a depth of 70 fm (128 m).

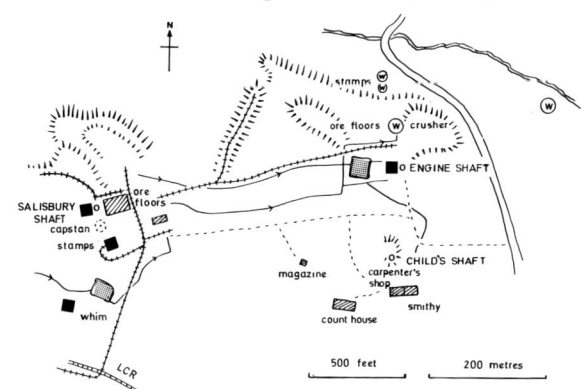

Plan of Marke Valley Mine.

MINEWORKERS

THE mining boom was well under way within a few years of the discoveries at South Caradon, and there was a great influx of mineworkers into the district. Already by 1844, there were 410 employed at South Caradon and 250 at West Caradon. Progress was apparently slower to the north of Caradon Hill, with only 30 at Phoenix Mine and 60 at Marke Valley. Numbers fluctuated from year to year, but in 1862, these were reported at the principal mines:

mine	mineworkers	copper ore (tons)	mine	mineworkers	copper ore (tons)
South Caradon	650	5,460	Marke Valley	300	4,821
West Caradon	470	3,090	Craddock Moor	250	1,879
Phoenix	460	4,628	East Caradon	180	5,265

Underground miners included **tutworkers,** who made a contract to break unpayable ground, such as shaft-sinking or driving new levels, while **tributers** worked only the lode, taking a share in the profit of ores sent to the surface or 'grass'. **Surface work,** mostly ore dressing, was undertaken by men, women and children. On the earlier copper mines the women (bal maidens) dressed the ores with small hammers, often in the open air. Later, dressing sheds were erected. In January 1862 at Phoenix Mine, employment at the surface was:

	MEN	BOYS	GIRLS
Tramming, filling and landing ores –	18	1	
Sundry labour –	22		
pitman; timbermen (4), watching Old Engine and Seccombe's Engine (2); attending to ore, coal, timber (2); working ore and coal waggons (3); attending to flat rods; surface work + postman; drying men's underground clothes (2); attending horses, etc; mason; cleaning flues and boiler, tending crusher (4).			
Smithery	7	2	
Carpentry and sawing	4		
Engineers	9		
working Old Engine and attending to Seccombe's and Ann's Engines; working Old Engine (2); working Seccombe's Engine (3); working Whim Engine (3)			
Dressing ores –	6	20	40
TOTAL:	66	23	40

These figures give a good indication of the type of surface work – in this case during a winter month so the figures are lower than normal (for example, an average 80 boys and 60 girls were employed in 1864). 128 miners were employed underground on tutwork; the rest were tributers.

MINING VILLAGES

THE Cornwall Great United management set about building cottages at Clanacombe to encourage some of their workforce to stay in an area remote from the main Cornish mining scene during the early uncertain days. However, the success of the new mines in the 1840s drew in hundreds of miners and their families from further west where the copper mines were starting to fail. This is seen dramatically in St Cleer parish, where the population rose from 982 in 1831 to 3,931 in 1861. All this brought a housing shortage and many of the present villages and hamlets owe their origins or development to the mines – Pensilva, Darite, Tremar, Caradon Town, Railway Terrace, Henwood and Cheesewring Railway (Minions). This was a boom time for Liskeard too. In 1856, John Allen wrote: 'the markets were thronged, the roads were worn into dangerous ruts, the dialect of the people grew more provincial and the singing tone of the west was imported with full effect.' The period was riotous, characterised by overcrowding and numerous drinking houses, one of the most notorious of which was known as the 'House of Blazes'. With the closure of the mines towards the end of the century, the population was already declining. Most villages retained an inn – for example the

Minions in the early twentieth century: an old postcard view.

Minions Primitive Methodist Chapel (now converted to a dwelling).

Crow's Nest Chapel (since demolished).

Cheesewring Inn at Henwood, but since closed. Minions could boast the Cheesewring Hotel and a temperance hotel, as well as two chapels.

Chapels are as much a part of the Cornish mining landscape as the villages and engine houses. Along with miners' cottages, most villages had a non-conformist chapel, such as in St Cleer, Tremar Coombe, Crow's Nest (Wesleyan), Minions (Primitive Methodist: 'PM') and Henwood. There was even a Bible Christian chapel – now a ruin – at Higher Stanbear on the track between Minions and Henwood. Some chapels are still in use, others have been converted to houses (as at Minions), or demolished. Their dates are significant, for example 1863 at Minions and Tremar Coombe: the height of the mining boom.

POSTSCRIPT: TWENTIETH-CENTURY MINING

STIMULATED by brief rises in the price of tin, all attempts to re-open mines in the twentieth century failed. The most impressive survival is at Phoenix United Mine. Its great engine house and associated buildings date from 1907-14, when the new Prince of Wales Shaft was sunk 1,193 ft (364 m). Inside the engine house, with its unusual square-based and tapered brick stack, are massive granite slabs with bolt holes for the 80-in pumping engine built by Holmans of Camborne. Boiler, winding and compressor houses are still intact, but roofless. Nearby, a large building was for horizontal stamps engines and boilers; the concrete loadings for stamps are outside. The dressing floors were to be laid out below, but the mine failed. A scheme in 1922 to drive a deep adit to de-water the Phoenix and Marke Valley mines came to nothing, and the Prince of Wales engine was scrapped in the 1930s.

South Phoenix Mine was re-opened in 1906-8 by the Cornish Consolidated Tin Mines Ltd. Concrete foundations for the winding gear and ancillary buildings of this period survive at Prosper Shaft (nearest Minions). Power was provided from a large generator house built beside the LCR near the old Rillaton bridge. Roofless for many years, this was converted into dwellings in about 1970. A last venture spent money at South Phoenix in 1920, and perhaps this was when

Houseman's engine house at South Phoenix Mine in 1969, shortly before the corrugated iron roof was removed.

Houseman's engine house was converted to a dwelling and offices – the building still had a corrugated iron roof until the late 1960s.

Subsequent activity has been on a much smaller scale. In 1936, Liskeard Minerals Ltd worked shallow trial shafts near Silver Valley, and erected a waterwheel in the valley below Wheal Jenkin. Canadians sunk a shaft for tin at Silver Valley in the Second World War, and finally International Mine Services of Toronto spent 1969 (a time of rising tin prices) digging pits and drilling to test the value of the lodes at depth around South Phoenix and Wheal Jenkin.

Sinking the Prince of Wales Shaft at the Phoenix United Mine, c. 1910: an old postcard view.

Shallow workings for tin at Silver Valley in 1936. Photo: H. G. Ordish.

WATER AND WATER POWER

ALTHOUGH blessed with ample rainfall, water for mining and streaming operations was precious high up on the moor; aerial photographs and closer inspection on the ground show numerous small water courses where the miners and streamers made every effort to capture and re-use surface water.

On the mines, water was required for ore dressing and the steam engines. For the latter, it was stored in an 'engine pool' close to the boiler and engine house, and many of these can be traced at South Caradon Mine (walk 3). A small leat contouring the hillside from the east brought water to a well-built pool at Pearce's Shaft, and surplus water descended, first to two pools at Sump Shaft and then a long reservoir pool. This still receives some water by a leat from Gonamena, while a second, dry, leat enters from the other end. The latter also supplied water to two pools at Jope's Shaft. No water was wasted, and the long reservoir supplied the copper ore dressing floors below and a 31-ft (9.4 m) diameter waterwheel for winding (a depression below the pool marks the wheelpit).

The Phoenix Leat is a carefully engineered watercourse 2¼ miles (3.6 km) long, most of which can be traced from a stream at Kilmar Lake on Twelve Men's Moor, then curving around the west slope of Langstone Down, through the Sharptor col and around the east side of Stowe's Hill to a point above the main site of Phoenix United Mine. It was already constructed or underway by 1841, as it appears on the Linkinhorne Tithe Map. Eventually it fed at least five pools on the main part of the mine, to provide water for steam engines and the copper and tin dressing floors. It was also supplemented by a leat from the direction of South Phoenix. Even after leaving the Phoenix Mine's dressing floors, water was used for treating the discharged tailings way down the valley at the Darley Stream Works and Oakbottom Stream Works (at Darleyford). The large dam across the Witheybrook tin work impounds a pool which supplied water via a leat (still traced) to two engine houses at West Phoenix Mine.

Waterpower was used wherever possible. It was first used for stamping the tin ore. For example, in 1837 there were six waterwheels working stamps in the Caradon Coombe valley, when a larger wheel was erected near Wheal Jenkin for pumping. Some very large diameter waterwheels operated in the district, including wheels of 50 ft (15.2 m) and 36 ft (11 m) for pumping and winding at North Phoenix Mine, 52 ft (15.8 m) and 40 ft (12.2 m) at Marke Valley Mine and a 60 ft (18.3 m) pumping wheel at Phoenix United Mine.

Three large masonry wheelpits survive in the area. In the woods below the breached dam wall in the Clanacombe valley, at SX 268727 is a spectacular wheelpit for a 60 ft x 2 ft (18.3 m x 0.6 m) waterwheel. The side walls are strengthened by external buttresses and a tunnel under a trackway behind the wheelpit shows the start of the 518 m line of flat rods which climbed to Old Sump Shaft on the Phoenix Mine. This pumping wheel was first mentioned in 1863. A wheelpit with room for a 50 ft x 4 ft (15.2 m x 1.2 m) stamping wheel is hidden in Caradon Coombe at SX 274716. Of unknown date, it may have been part of Dunsley Wheal Phoenix Mine. The third wheelpit is visible from the track up from Crow's Nest, on the west side of the Seaton stream at SX 264695. It is aligned with an old shaft 110 m upslope, and probably contained the 40-ft (12.2 m) wheel reported pumping at the small East Wheal Agar Mine in 1846. Visitors to Golitha Falls (outside the Minions Moor area) cannot fail to notice the two large wheelpits of Wheal Victoria beside the river.

A MINING GLOSSARY

ACCOUNT or COUNT HOUSE – The mine's office and usually a large building on the richer mines. That at Phoenix United has a first floor bay window from which pitches in the mine were auctioned to the tributers on setting days.

ADIT – A level cut into a hillslope from a valley bottom to drain a mine. Water was always a problem and pumping became necessary when the mines became deeper. Waterwheels were used for pumping on the small workings, but the larger mines required a steam engine.

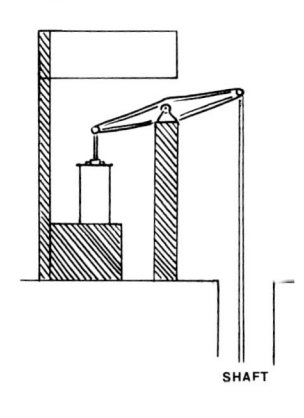

BEAM ENGINE – PUMPING – Usually larger and more powerful, and erected beside the shaft. The outdoor end of the beam was attached a timber rod which worked a series of pumps as it rose and fell in the shaft, forcing water from the very bottom of the mine up to the surface or adit (drainage) level. To counteract the weight of the pump rod, 'balance bobs' were placed at the surface (seen at the Prince of Wales Shaft) and down the shaft.

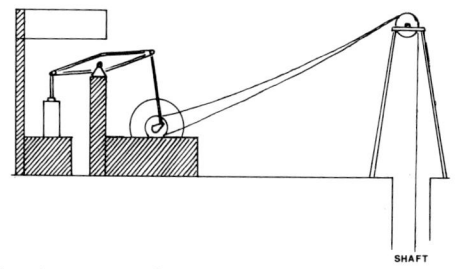

BEAM ENGINE – WINDING – Beam engines for winding (whims) were attached by means of a sweep rod and crank to a winding drum set on a 'loading' in front of the bob wall. Where they survive, the gap for the drum and flywheel can be recognised. Winding engines were set back from the shaft to allow the ropes to reach the top of the head frame.

81

East–west section along the principal area of workings on the main lode of Phoenix United Mine, showing shafts, levels and mined-out areas or 'stopes' (shaded).

Round buddle at East Caradon Mine.

BEAM ENGINE – STAMPING – As with the whim engines, the same crank mechanism was used to drive stamps for crushing tin ores. A revolving horizontal cam-shaft raised lifters with heavy iron shoes or 'stamps'. When released, these fell and crushed the tin ore beneath to a fine sand, which was then processed on the dressing floors. Stamps were very loud and could be heard many miles away. Earlier stamping mills worked in the same way, but were smaller and powered by a waterwheel.

BLACK TIN – Tin ore prepared ready for smelting.

BUDDLE – A circular pit, about 6 m diameter, with a convex base and centre stone. Fine stamped tin ore was fed in at the centre with water, while rotating brushes helped spread the material. The lighter waste was washed outwards leaving a heavier tin concentrate in the centre. When full, the buddle was carefully dug out.

DRESSING FLOOR – An extensive area at the mine surface where ores were processed to remove the waste. On a tin mine, the ores were stamped and separated in circular buddles. Finer material was processed in concave buddles and the finest 'slimes' concentrated in round tables and long 'rag frames'. Examples of dressing floors can be traced at South Phoenix Mine, Wheal Jenkin and in the valley below

Phoenix United Mine. Dressing copper ores employed more labour, especially girls and children who first sorted and spalled (broke) the ores by hand. The 'bal maidens' used pointed cobbing hammers to remove the waste from the betters ores, and flat bucking hammers to reduce the ores to the size of a pea. Powered crushing rollers replaced bucking, although ores were still picked by hand. Poorer ores were stamped. Cobbled ore floors can be seen in the valley bottom at South Caradon Mine.

ENGINE HOUSE – Steam beam engines for pumping, winding and stamping were erected in the tall engine houses so characteristic of Cornwall. Inside may be found the granite bedstones with bolt holes to take the great cylinder, the diameter of which was always measured in inches, giving the size of the engine. In one wall is the large cylinder arch (through which the engine was brought into the house), while opposite is a lower and thicker 'bob wall' which supported the heavy beam. Often overlooked, there was a boilerhouse alongside; being less substantial, only traces usually remain. A brick-topped chimney stack was built onto a corner of the engine house, at the end of the boiler house or freestanding. The largest mines had many steam engines, which had to be supplied with coal via the LCR. For example, at their closures South Caradon Mine had 12 large and four smaller engines in 1885 and Phoenix United had 12 engines in 1898.

FLAT ROD – A long rod (supported on posts with 'dolly wheels') for transmitting power for pumping, usually from a waterwheel, whereby a crank converted rotary motion to horizontal through the rod and then to vertical in a shaft by means of an 'angle bob'.

Horse whim round at Webb's Shaft, South Caradon Mine.

HORIZONTAL ENGINE – Some engine houses contained engines with a horizontal cylinder – usually for winding. Such buildings are distinct from the taller beam engine houses and a good example stands upslope from Sump Shaft on South Caradon Mine (walk 3).

HORSE WHIM – For winding at shallower shafts. A large winding drum was pivoted vertically on a 'mellior stone' set in the ground at the centre of a circle. A rope on the drum travelled over a head frame and wheels into an adjacent shaft. Ore and waste rock were raised in kibbles by a horse walking around the circle while harnessed to a bar attached to the drum. The best examples of whim rounds are at South Phoenix Mine (walk 1) and South Caradon Mine (walk 3).

LEAT – An artificial water course bringing water onto a mine for engines or dressing floors.

LODE – The main ore body, vertical or inclined, varying considerably in width and containing tin and copper minerals alongside unwanted 'gangue' minerals such as quartz. Often marked at the surface outcrop by a long line of shafts and test pits.

NAMES OF MINES AND SHAFTS – The rich South, West and East Caradon Mines spawned others in the neighbourhood with the magic name 'Caradon' to attract investors. Such were Glasgow Caradon Consols (the most successful), Caradon Consols, Caradon United, Great Caradon, New Caradon, New South Caradon and New West Caradon. Rather hopeful, was Great North Caradon, a lead and silver prospect in Advent parish on the other side of Bodmin Moor! The other great name was Phoenix, as seen at Dunsley Wheal Phoenix, East Phoenix, North Phoenix, South Phoenix and West Phoenix. To get the best of both names, a zinc mine in North Hill parish was called Caradon and Phoenix Consols.

  Shafts – were named after mine owners, managers or mine captains. So, for example, Clymo's, Rule's, Holman's and Kittow's Shafts at South Caradon were named after the managers Peter Clymo, William Rule and John Holman, and secretary Thomas Kittow. There are Seccombe's Shafts at Phoenix and East Caradon – James Seccombe and his son were managers here – and at Marke Valley in the 1850s and 60s.

OLD MEN – A term given to earlier miners or streamers of distant and unknown date.

SHAFTS – Pumping, winding and air shafts were vertical or inclined to follow a lode, or sunk to intercept it at depth. Ores and waste were hauled in 'kibbles'; miners used ladderways to descend and ascend, although there was a 'man-engine' at South Caradon before haulage cages were introduced. The depths of mines were always measured by the fathom (1.8 m). The deepest shafts below adit in the district were on South Caradon Mine, at Sump Shaft, 250 fm (457 m), and Rule's North Shaft, 230 fm (421 m), while Phoenix United Mine had Seccombe's Shaft, 225 fm (412 m), and the Prince of Wales Shaft, 199 fm (364 m). Shaft sinking and mining were achieved by hand-boring and blasting, and it was only in later years that compressed air drills were introduced. As a measure of the Victorian miners' skill, it is a sobering thought that two lengths of Caradon Hill's great television mast could be thrust down South Caradon Mine's Sump Shaft before reaching the bottom!

STOPE – The part of the mineral lode which is mined out underground, worked upwards from a level (overhand stoping) or downwards (underhand stoping).

STREAMWORKS – Some small valley streamworks operated in the twentieth century. Other types were more extensive, treating the waste and tailings sent down from mines above, such as the Darley Stream Works and Oakbottom Stream Works below Phoenix United Mine.

RAILWAYS

THE many upper branches of the former Liskeard & Caradon Railway can be followed throughout this small area. The railway was built to serve the copper mines and granite quarries, and several of the shareholders and management were involved in mining (for example, the first directors included Peter and James Clymo of South Caradon Mine and John Allen of West Caradon Mine). Within a few years of the discovery of the rich South Caradon copper mine, the use of packhorses and the poor state of the local roads were found to be totally inadequate for the increased heavy traffic. An Act was passed and the railway opened in March 1846 to Moorswater near Liskeard. This was the terminus of the Liskeard & Looe Union Canal, upon which ores and granite were carried to the quays at Looe, the copper ore for shipment to South Wales for smelting and the granite to many destinations around Britain.

The LCR was standard-gauge, with rails laid on granite sleeper blocks. It was horse-drawn on the uphill journey, bringing coal, timber and other stores to the mines, while gravity was used to send the ore and granite laden trucks back down to the canal basin at Moorswater. At the upper end of the line, there were two branches: a short one to South Caradon Mine and a longer one which ascended the Gonamena incline and passed through what is now Minions to Cheesewring Quarry. There was also a short incline to West Caradon Mine.

From Minions, the Kilmar Railway was built in 1858 by quarrying interests to develop granite works further out on the moor. It contoured around the hillside from Minions to Sharptor, where there was a siding. Beyond Sharptor, the course of the tramway climbed onto Twelve Men's Moor, where there were branches to granite workings at Kilmar Tor and Bearah Tor. Steam locomotives were introduced after 1860 when the railway was extended as the Liskeard & Looe Railway alongside the canal all the way to Looe. Heavier rails were laid and some alterations were made to accommodate the three locomotives named 'Caradon', 'Cheesewring' and 'Kilmar', but the Gonamena incline prevented them from reaching Minions. In 1861,

The Liskeard & Caradon Railway and its branches.

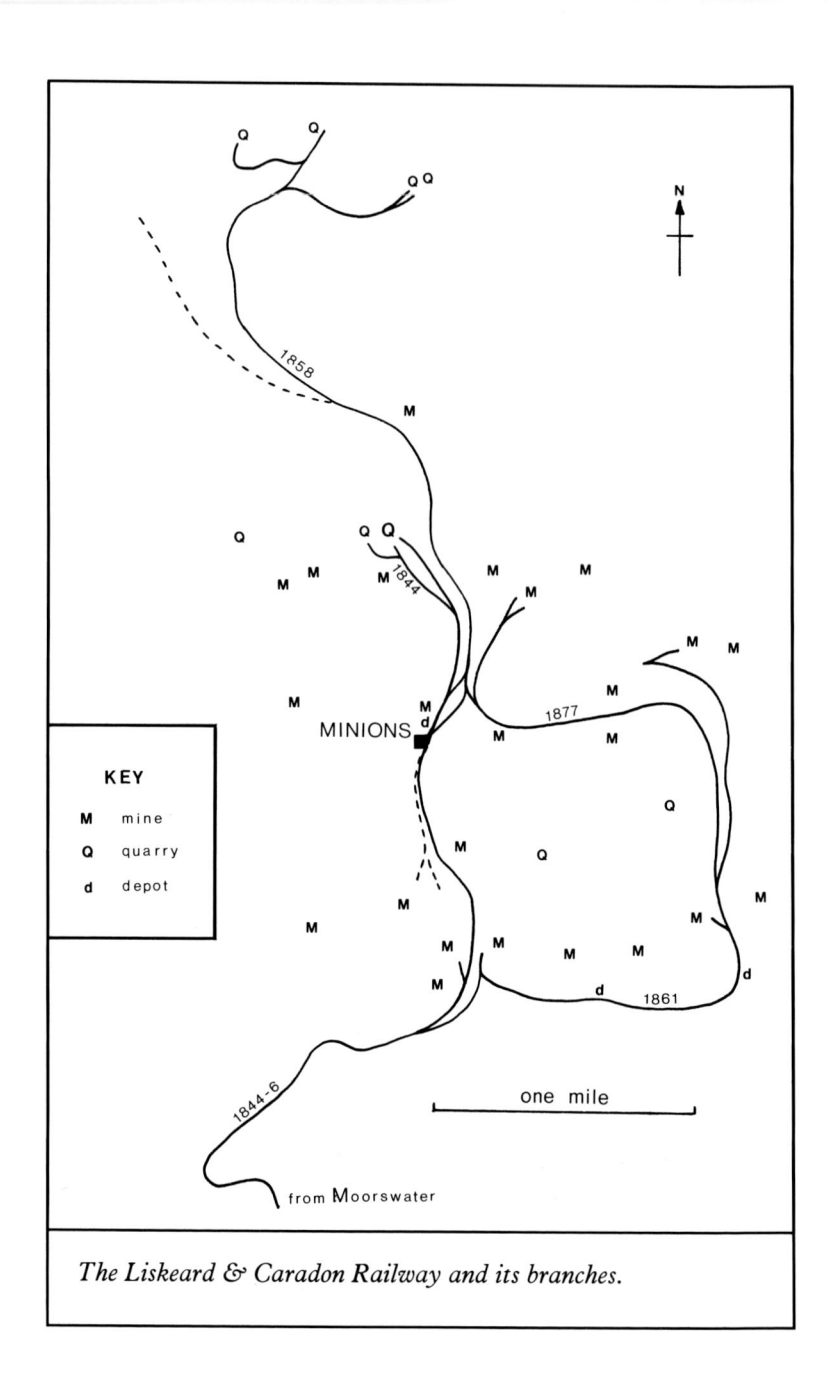

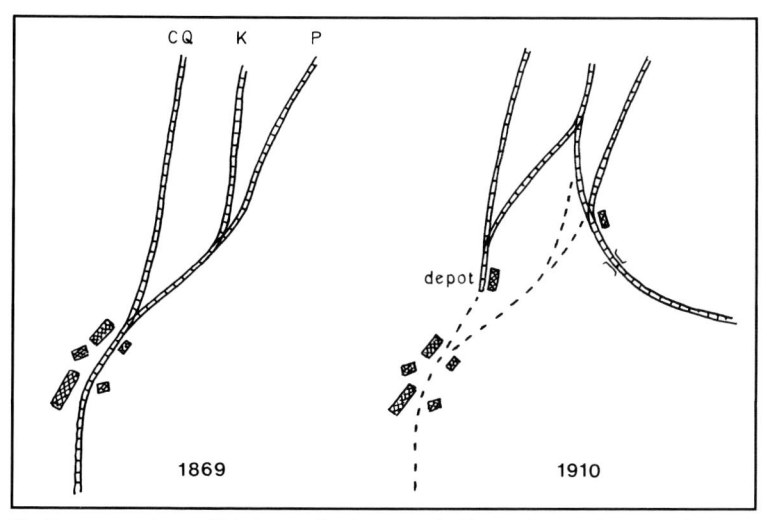

Railway mania at Minions: the layout of all tracks can be traced.

the line was extended from a reversal at South Caradon to Tokenbury Corner, where there are still traces of a depot beside the road. There was a siding to East Caradon Mine. A longer branch was opened in August 1877 to Marke Valley Mine, and three months later the main line (known as the Kilmar Junction Railway) was carried around the north side of Caradon Hill to meet the existing railway at Minions, and the old Gonamena section fell out of use.

Behind Minions, a complex of junctions and reversals enabled locomotives to join the line to Cheesewring Quarry. There was also a branch to Phoenix United Mine dating from 1869 (now followed by the Henwood road) and a short siding to serve the 1906 re-working of Prosper Shaft at South Phoenix Mine. The foundations of the former Rillaton Depot, or store, and its platform can be located here. The track which leads to Cheesewring enters the quarry through a cutting made in 1871 when the quarry was deepened, but the original track and its sleeper blocks can be traced a little higher up.

Out on the Kilmar Railway (purchased by the LCR in 1877), an Act was passed in 1882 to build a 5½-mile Northern Extension from Sharptor to Trewint, with later more ambitious plans to extend branches to Camelford and Launceston. Some work was done and the course of this line from Sharptor can be seen following the

Witheybrook valley, with embankments, cuttings and at least one bridge. The unfinished line, which was never laid, ends in an abandoned cutting after 2¾ miles (4.4 km).

Other branches included an unfinished line from Minions towards Craddock Moor (the course survives), while a Gold Diggings Quarry branch was planned in 1882 but never started.

During its lifetime the LCR carried thousands of tons of ore, coal, granite, timber, etc. A peak year was 1868, with 61,863 tons of goods carried. Open trucks, mostly of 6 tons capacity, were used but there were some special heavier trucks for granite. Traffic declined rapidly after the closure of mines, especially South Caradon in 1885. For a period passengers were carried at their own risk – being charged for an umbrella or hat before the issue of a 'free' pass. The open trucks were used to carry some excursion traffic, which included temperance parties and school parties. These were usually horse-drawn, but about 160 members of the British Association, during their 1877 meeting in Plymouth, were carried in ten trucks behind a locomotive to visit the Caradon and Phoenix Mines, the Cheesewring and other attractions, before returning by gravity.

The LCR was bought in 1909 by the Great Western Railway, to which it had been joined at Liskeard since 1901. The railway from Moorswater closed on 1st January 1917 and, it is said, the rails were lifted and shipped out to help the war in France. The line in the picturesque Looe valley survives as a passenger service.

MOORSTONE CUTTING

THE moorstones (clitter) lying scattered around the tors have been taken by man since Neolithic times. They were removed for burial chambers (see the large stones of Trethevy Quoit), stone circles, and house building, but there is little evidence for stone dressing at that time. In the medieval period many moorstones were cut up and carried away for church building – see, for example, the dressed granite in the parish churches of Linkinhorne and St Cleer or North Hill. Over the years other stones were removed for buildings, lintels, gateposts, millstones, kerbstones, paving, and many other uses. Even after quarrying began in the 1840s, moorstones were still exploited down to the mid-twentieth century. Thousands of tons must have gone, indicated by pits or remaining moorstones bearing stone-cutters' marks.

There are three directions for cleaving granite, none easy to recognise and each with increasing difficulty: 1. Capping or Quartering – horizontal, parallel with the 'floor'. 2. Cleaving – vertical, in the general direction of the feldspar crystals. 3. Tough Way – vertical, against the 'grain'.

The early stone-cutters used the 'wedge and groove' method, whereby grooves were chiselled out in a line so that wedges could be inserted to split the granite. The method dates back at least to Roman times, although examples on Bodmin Moor must be medieval or later. Examples are found just north of the Rillaton Barrow, near Gold Diggings and among the very summit rocks of Stowe's Hill. A number must be the work of the legendary Daniel Gumb and it would be nice to think that the neater ones are his. The easiest to find are the lines of abandoned grooves – never split for some reason – but it requires practice to recognise the faint half-grooves along split edges.

The more efficient 'plug and feather' method was introduced after 1800. There is widespread evidence for its use, with many stones bearing split faces and lines of holes about 8 cm deep and 8 cm apart along the top. The holes were made with a hand-held borer or a 'jumper'. The latter was an iron rod about 1.7 m long with two cutting ends and a swelling in the middle for weight, and was 'jumped' up and

Grooves cut in a moorstone below the Cheeswring. Scale: 1ft. (305mm).

down on the desired spot. To split the rock, steel plugs were placed between thin half-round plates ('feathers') in the holes and driven home. Similar marks can be seen on the blocks at quarries in the area. Much activity took place on the gentler ground at the foot of the steep west slope of Stowe's Hill, where stones were worked by individuals subcontracted to supply the operators of Cheesewring Quarry. After a moorstone had been selected and split into the approximate dimensions required, it was rough 'scappled' and squared with a pick. A 'patent axe' (thin steel blades in a frame fastened to a handle) was then used to give the stone finer dimensions, starting at a carefully squared edge. Several roughed-out and partly squared blocks lie on the moor in various stages of readiness. Some almost complete works were abandoned for some reason, perhaps the sudden appearance of a hidden crack.

Much of the granite-working at Kilmar was among the moorstones rather than actual quarrying. Around 2,500 tons of granite was carried away each year on the railway in 1859-63, and up to 7,367 tons in 1864 when John and William Freeman took over the sett. In May 1868, nearly 80 men were at work on the moorstones below Kilmar Tor, preparing them for works at Portsmouth Dockyard and forts at Spithead and the Thames. There were another 60 men working on the moorstones and new quarry at Bearah Tor. 'Crab' winches were used to 'draw the stones into their proper places' below Kilmar Tor, and 14 substantial loading ramps beside the old railway track testify to the extent of activity.

Tool sharpening would have been a problem at this remote spot had the stone-cutters not been served by two blacksmith's shops. The first was built at the time of the first lease near the railway and the source of a small stream (Kilmar Lake). A smaller smithy was provided beside the railway much closer to Kilmar Tor. By 1875, work had virtually ceased.

A shaped and abandoned moorstone west of the Cheesewring.

GRANITE QUARRYING

THE quality of the Bodmin Moor granite is such that it was sought in the nineteenth century for many civil engineering works, public buildings and monuments. Cheesewring Quarry is described here in more detail, being one of the largest granite quarries in Cornwall and a site where most evidence is typical of all others. Work first started when a lease was granted in 1845 to John Trethewey, a Plymouth granite merchant. A cutting for a tramway leading around to loading platforms and a small quarry on the west side of the hill may be of an early date. Quarried granite was carried on the Liskeard & Caradon Railway (the upper part was opened in 1844) down to Moorswater and then by canal to Looe, where there was a large crane for loading ships. The Cheesewring Granite Co. displayed a 9.1 m high Ionic column at the 1851 Great Exhibition. The shaft was worked at the quarry and the base and capital finished at the firm's wharf at Lambeth. The column now stands in a field near Stroud, Gloucestershire.

In 1853, the firm was taken over by Messrs Tregelles and Crouch who developed the quarry and built the Kilmar Railway. In 1864, the Cheesewring Granite Co Ltd came into the hands of John and William Freeman (later, John Freeman & Sons), the foremost granite quarriers in Cornwall. By then there was a granite workyard at Moorswater and railway all the way to Looe. In May 1868 'upwards of 100 stalwart men and boys' were at work in the quarry. One gang was clearing overburden from an unquarried part, while others were high up on the face, boring holes for blasting. The floor of the quarry was occupied by masons, working on stones of 5–12 tons. This was a particularly busy time with work for government fortifications and dockyards.

The faces at Cheesewring Quarry show how use was made of the natural joints in the granite – vertical (two directions) and horizontal (often called the 'bed' but an incorrect term). To obtain the largest possible blocks, holes up to 10 cm diameter were bored down to the horizontal joint with long chisel-ended borers struck by heavy hammers, and just sufficient black powder was rammed home and fired to lift the mass from the 'bed' without shattering the stone. The

Developments at Cheesewring Quarry, 1870–1980.

96

Cheesewring Quarry in about 1910: an old postcard view.

remaining half of these vertical boreholes can be seen on the rock face. Masses up to 1,000 tons were quarried in this way.

Large quarried blocks were broken down with plugs and feathers (see 'Moorstone Cutting'), a method still used for secondary breaking in granite quarries today, although pneumatic drills are used. Deeper holes ensured a more accurate split. To bore a line of holes, the quarrymen stood on a block and worked in turn, the different tones of their jumpers making a distinct sound. On 10th March 1863, there was a holiday at the quarry to celebrate the wedding of the Duke of Cornwall to Princess Alexandra. Banners were fixed to the cranes and several peals were rung by the quarrymen in sets of six jumpers. They kept time and produced a 'most musical' sound. Such 'ringing the jumper' might explain the curious holes pitting the surface of the eastern tor on Stowe's Hill.

Masons shaped the blocks in the open, but open-fronted sheds or 'bankers' were later erected to give them shelter. More detailed work took place at Moorswater, where there were steam saws and polishers.

Granite blocks up to 20 tons were lifted by three timber cranes which were supported by chain or wire guys from anchor points around the edge of the quarry. The bases of a large lattice steel crane and its steam winding engine can be seen inside the quarry. This crane

The East Cornwall Bank (now Barclays) on the Parade, Liskeard, was faced in granite from Cheesewring Quarry in 1851.

Splitting a granite block at Bearah Quarry in 1974. The quarryman is using a sledge hammer to strike in succession the 'plugs' which have been inserted between 'feathers' in a line of drilled holes. Such a method has been in use on the moors for nearly 200 years.

was used for loading railway trucks. Waste was trammed out onto the massive tips. Because only the largest blocks were sought for 'dimension' stone, waste tips of large angular blocks are a major feature of this type of quarrying (unfortunately disturbed by modern stone-taking at Cheesewring in 1984).

Cheesewring Quarry was deepened in the 1870s and the railway entered through a narrow cutting at a lower level. However, output had declined by 1917 when the LCR closed and little granite was quarried thereafter. Some rails and sleeper blocks survive inside the quarry. Outside the entrance, between two waste tips, are the walls of the first blacksmith's shop, which may pre-date the quarry. The magazine for storing gunpowder is 70 m south of the quarry entrance. Below the quarry track are the ruins of Cheesewring Cottages and their garden plots, a terrace built by the Freemans for their workers in 1864. They were inhabited until after the Second World War, but demolished by 1950.

Among its many uses, granite from Cheesewring can be found in the East Cornwall Bank (now Barclays), Liskeard; Moorswater viaduct; Albert Memorial, Guards' Memorial, base of Wellington's tomb in London; Thames Embankment; forts at Spithead, Thames, Medway and Plymouth Breakwater; Fastnet Lighthouse, Great Basses Lighthouse in Ceylon (Sri Lanka); Putney, Westminster and Tower Bridges; Devonport and Portsmouth Dockyards; docks in London, Birkenhead, Southampton, Calcutta and Copenhagen; breakwaters at Alderney, Dover and Portland.

Other quarries in the area were worked downwards because they were not restricted by the requirements of a railway. Now abandoned, they are flooded with deep water. Such are Gold Diggings Quarry and Caradon Quarry, both worked by the Liskeard firm of Joseph Sweet & Sons until 1931 and the early 1960s respectively. Some stone was shaped at the quarries but much was taken by road to their workyard in Liskeard, mainly for building and monumental work. Twentieth-century quarries included blacksmith's shops and power plant, such as oil engines, to work compressors for rock drills and cranes, or saws and polishers. Traces of all these may survive.

The quarries out at Bearah and Kilmar are of interest. Despite the masses of moorstones worked at the latter, a branch from the Kilmar Railway around to a small quarry on the north side of the tor was laid in 1879 on sleeper blocks from the old Gonamena incline. Work ceased soon after. There was a brief revival just after the Second World War, with small scale quarrying by R.C.H. and S.H. Bassett for monumental and other uses at the south and east end of Kilmar Tor. At Bearah Tor, the old quarries were reopened and enlarged after 1948 by Messrs Piper for monumental and building work. The site is still in use and includes an old crane from Launceston railway station.

DANIEL GUMB

DANIEL GUMB was the most celebrated character to inhabit the moors, and is best known for his home among the rocks at Cheesewring, which was a very remote spot in those days. He was born on 14th April 1703 in Linkinhorne parish and was noted for his reserve and great love of reading and study as a child. His main occupation of stone-cutting brought him to the hill at Cheesewring, where on the southern slopes he found a slightly inclined block measuring 10 m by 3 m, which he made the roof of his 'house' by excavating beneath and lining the sides with stone, cemented with lime. Channels were cut in the roof stone, to carry off and collect rainwater, and the dwelling was divided into 'rocky cells and sleeping rooms adjoining, of very narrow dimensions'. In front, on the south side, was an enclosure within a low wall. This was where Gumb lived free of rent with his bride Florence Brokinshaw in 1743. She bore him a large family, although many died young. He had been been married before, in 1735 to Thomazine Roberts, who died, perhaps in childbirth, a year later. That she too lived here, is suggested by the stone carved 'D. Gumb 1735'. There is a hint of an even earlier marriage, in 1732, to one Joan of whom little is known.

The top of the rock served Gumb as an observatory from which he viewed the movements of the stars at night. On the surface he carved mathematical diagrams, one of which survives. He gained a reputation as the 'Mountain Philosopher' and received a number of distinguished visitors, such as William Cookworthy who is best known for his discovery of china clay.

There are various accounts of Daniel Gumb, but the main source was written nearest the time by John Bond of Chacewater, in a letter dated 18th October 1814 to the editor of the ***West Briton*** newspaper. In this he describes how as a young man Gumb became celebrated in the neighbouring parishes for his mathematical knowledge. 'But neither his studious habits nor his reserve could exempt our philosopher from the shafts of Cupid; in the very morning of manhood, he became enamoured of a buxom lass belonging to his native parish, and after some time in courtship, he made her his wife.'

He took her to live in his rocky house which 'became his chapel also, and he was never known to descend from the craggy mountain on which it stood, to attend his parish church, or any other place of worship . . . "for why," as the good woman used to express herself, "Daniel was a far enow better scolard than the Passen was." '

The most fanciful account was by Rev R.S. Hawker of Morwenstow in which he claims to to have found fragments of Gumb's diary, treasured by his descendants, when he visited the area in the 1830s. For example, on the fly-leaves of an old account book, he found recorded in a formal and painful handwriting:

'June 23rd, 1764. Today, at bright noon, as I was at my work upon the moor, I looked up and saw all at once a stranger standing on the turf, just above my block. He was dressed like an old picture I remember in the windows of St Neot's church, in a long brown garment, with a girdle; and his head was uncovered and grizzled with long hair. He spoke to me in a low clear voice, "Daniel, that work is hard!" I wondered that he should know my name, and I answered, "Yes, sir; but I am used to it, and don't mind it, for the sake of the faces at home." Then he said, sounding his words like a psalm, "Man goeth forth to his work and to his labour until the evening; when will it be night with Daniel Gumb?" I began to feel queer; it seemed to me that there was something awful about the unknown man. I even shook. Then he said again, "Fear nothing. The happiest man in all the earth is he that wins his daily bread by his daily sweat, if he will but fear God and do no man wrong." I bent down my head like any one confounded, and I greatly wondered who this strange appearance

One of only two known plans of Gumb's House, made in 1870, showing the 'little walled curtilage and garden on the south side.'

Daniel Gumb's House today.

could be. He was not like a preacher, for he looked me full in the face; nor a bit like a parson, for he seemed very meek and kind . . . But when I looked up he was gone, and that clear out of my sight, on the bare wide moor suddenly. I only wish that I had gone forward at once and felt him with my hand and found out if he was a real man or only a resemblance. What could it mean?'

Gumb died in 1776, when (to quote Bond) 'death, which alike seizes on the philosopher and the fool, at length found out the retreat of Daniel Gumb, and lodged him in a house more narrow than which he had dug for himself.'

His son John continued his father's trade of stone-cutting but found himself a more comfortable house elsewhere and abandoned 'Gumb's House'. By 1851, two John Gumbs (grandson and great grandson?) were copper miners living at Henwood.

Although it was understood that 'Gumb's Rocks' would be respected, it was destroyed without warning when Cheesewring Quarry was extended in 1873. The true site is somewhere out in the quarry, suspended about 12 m in the air! A portion of the roof was saved by the quarrymen, and is said to have been moved three times before being re-erected on its present location just outside the quarry. 'Daniel Gumb's Cave' is really only a fragment of the original roof

103

Moorstone carvings near the south end of the demolished Cheesewring Cottages are probably crude imitations of Daniel Gumb's work.

slab (with one surviving Pythagoran diagram and two cut channels), as drill marks at the back show how plugs and feathers were used to cut off this end of the block. These marks are also on the supporting stones, and because this splitting method dates from after 1800, they are a give-away clue that this is a reconstruction. Anyone wondering how Gumb and his family could have lived in such a small 'cave' now knows the answer! Alongside is a stone carved 'D. Gumb 1735', perhaps part of a doorpost said to have been in the bedroom.

That Daniel Gumb was a competent stone carver is confirmed by a very fine slate tombstone of c.1744 placed against the east wall of St Melor's church, Linkinhorne. At the foot of this stone is inscribed 'Cut by Daniel Gumb'. There is also the carving on the roof of his house, but similar diagrams near the demolished terrace of Cheesewring Cottages seem too crude to be his work and could be imitations. Some of the neatly cut grooves around the base of the Cheesewring and summit rocks may be his – those close to an abandoned millstone or cider press are particularly neat. Gumb's mathematical knowledge gained him part-time employment as a surveyor, and a plan he made of walls on the edge of Twelve Men's Moor in 1768 is preserved in the County Record Office.

BOUNDARY STONES AND MARKERS

A GREAT variety of granite marker stones can be found around the area, particularly on 'Cheesewring Moor'. The most impressive are the 2 m high tapering obelisks marking the bounds of Rillaton Manor erected by the Duchy of Cornwall in 1846. One of the four faces has a neatly carved individual number above 'RIL 1846'. Stones numbered 1-8 are concentrated around Minions and the higher Witheybrook area (see walk 1). There is a long gap before stones 9 and 10, which are close together way out on Twelve Mens Moor (walk 4), while '11 RIL 1846' is carved on top of a rock at the west end of Bearah Tor.

Other stones mark the boundaries of mining and quarrying setts – it was important to mark out the exact boundary of a mine, to ensure a neighbour did not encroach on another's potential mineral wealth (it was more difficult to survey underground of course). Square stones 'WB 1 – 4' west of the Cheesewring belong to the old Witheybrook Mine, while on the east side of Stowe's Hill, near the course of the Kilmar Railway, a stone 'PX 1' refers to the Phoenix Mine. On Caradon Hill there are tall round-headed stones, 'EC' (East Caradon Mine) and 'MV' (Marke Valley Mine) – see walk 3.

Well cut boundary stones also mark granite-working setts. On Cheesewring Moor, the stones 'BS C 1' and 'BS C 2' date from March 1864 and mark the southern boundary of the 103 ha. Cheesewring Granite Sett. The second is carved beneath the 'WB 2' stone overlooking the Witheybrook tin works. Stones from an earlier and larger sett of 1845, granted to Trethewey, Clogg & Co., were erected at Wardbrook ('CW 1') and Witheybrook Marsh ('CW 2').

On Twelve Men's Moor, the boundary stones of the Kilmar Granite Sett (356 ha.) also date from 1864. Stones 'BS K 1 – 4' run from near Sharp Tor across Langstone Downs to Kilmar Lake (walk 4), while stones 5 and 8 lie in or beside the Witheybrook stream. Stone 6 is against a field wall in the shallow col near Hawk's Tor, but 7 has not been located.

There are also stones belonging to the railway. A boundary stone, 'LCR', stands at the top of the Gonamena incline (walk 3), but most are milestones. For example, there are five markers, '1', '2', '3', '1M'

Quarry limits: carved symbols indicating the boundary to protect the rocky tors of Stowe's Hill from the Cheesewring quarrymen. Top: circled cross of 1845. Bottom: fleur-de-lis mark of 1864.

The carved number '4' on a rock at Bearah Tor is a marker dating from 1856. Kilmar Tor is beyond. Photo: J. Berry.

and '1', at quarter-mile intervals along the track of the Kilmar Railway from Minions. Further milestones can be seen beside the loop around the north side of Caradon Hill, with '15', '15¾' and '16' giving the distance in miles from Looe Quay.

More crudely carved stones around the moors include parish boundaries (which also used prominent boulders or blocks).

While the granite quarriers cut and took moorstones, the terms of their leases did not permit them to destroy the tors at Cheesewring, Sharp Tor, Bearah and Kilmar. Remarkably, in an area much scarred by nineteenth-century tin streaming, mining and granite quarrying, the rocky summits were protected by the Duchy of Cornwall. Under the terms of the 1845 lease at Cheesewring, seven circles containing a cross were cut on conspicuous rocks to define the protected area, 40 yd (36.5 m) west and north, and 20 yd (18.3 m) east of Stowe's Pound and 44 yd (40.2 m) south of the Cheesewring on the south side of the hill. No act was to be done 'which may lead to the injury or defacing of the Druidical remains or natural curiosities existing either on the Cheesewring Hill or elsewhere.' Protective clauses were also written into the leases of the Kilmar Granite Sett. In 1856, the boundary numbers 1–31 and 1–21 were to be cut around the rocks of Kilmar Tor and Bearah Tor respectively, while no stones were to be taken from within 100 yd (91.4 m) of the base of Sharp Tor and 30 yd (27.4 m) of East Point Tor.

Some of these early marks survive, but when the Freemans negotiated a new lease in 1864, 17 'fleur-de-lis' marks were to be cut around the hilltop, although now only 14 yd (12.8 m) south of the Cheesewring. When the Freemans combined the Cheesewring and Kilmar Setts at the same date, the protected areas remained, except that 54 and 32 fleur-de-lis marks were cut around Kilmar and Bearah Tors. As before, these marks were to be kept clearly painted so the stone-cutters would be in no doubt of their location. The paint has long since vanished but these marks still arouse curiosity. They are like some primeval monster's footprint in the once molten granite! With patience, or armed with Jim Berry's excellent little guide, a search makes an entertaining outing on all three summits.

One of the many boundary stones found on the moors. This one is on Cheesewring Moor.

ROCK CLIMBING

VISITORS to the Minions Moor may see rock climbers in action, especially on the great faces at Cheesewring Quarry and even on the rocky tors, where there are many short but difficult routes.

Shepherds and stockmen working on the moor must have climbed the easier tors since earliest times. Maybe Daniel Gumb had a scramble or two near his home at Cheesewring, but the first record of a 'climb' was an ascent of Kilmar Tor made by Thomas Bond and a friend on 6th August 1802. Their ascent of the 'eastern turret' was described in gripping terms by Bond, concluding 'the next thing to be considered was how we should get down again . . . and I believe nothing will ever induce me to pay a second visit to the top of this rock.' The first people to climb routinely as a pastime on the moorland tors were Sir Bertrand Jerram and D. G. Romanis. They may even have climbed at Cheesewring Quarry in the 1920s when it was still being worked, so their routes have probably since been destroyed and carried away.

The first serious modern climbing occurred at Cheesewring Quarry in the 1960s when young local climbers realised the quarry's potential and recorded over 30 routes on the main faces. The two boldest climbs of this period, named 'Eyefull Tower' and 'High Noon', are both graded Extremely Severe and tackle the steep 120 ft (36 m) face just left of the central overhang. Much of this early climbing development was made by members of the Minions Group. There was less activity in the 1970s, but since the mid-1980s, many new and very hard routes have been made by the next generation of climbers, who turned their attention to the lower surrounding walls of the quarried amphitheatre. This is the realm of the 'sports climber' who tackles short, extremely hard routes which are climbed for their technical difficulty.

Cheesewring Quarry is now the most important climbing location in inland Cornwall. There is shelter on the shorter faces at most times of the year although the rock can become very wet and greasy in winter. There are climbs here of all standards and some smaller cliff faces are ideal for teaching the techniques of climbing and abseiling. All routes are given names by the climber who made the first ascent;

Climbers on 'Eyefull Tower' a tough sixties route in the Extremely Severe Grade, climbed in traditional style on the main face of Cheesewring Quarry, and requiring steady nerves.

Khyber Wall is a climb from the 1970s on which pitons were used for aid – the climber pulled up on them! Today modern training and protection techniques allow a 'free' ascent using only the holds on the rock.

they are also graded according to their difficulty, from 'Moderate' through to 'Very Difficult', 'Very Severe' and 'Extremely Severe' ('E'). The highest grades have a number to indicate the degree of severity, such as 'E6'. Ropes are for protection only, passed through karabiners with slings attached to pitons, nuts inserted in small cracks or fixed bolts, and held by the climber's partner.

Climbers have been active in quarries elsewhere. Gold Diggings Quarry, across the valley to the west of Cheesewring has short climbs of all standards above its two flooded workings, but the smaller Caradon Quarry is less promising.

Of the tors, the most famous is the Cheesewring itself, which can be climbed with the aid of a rope or shoulder on the upper side (Victorian photographs witness parties posing on the top) but experts are able to climb it unaided. Other tors on Stowe's Hill offer a problem or two. Out on the moor, to the north of Cheesewring, Sharp Tor (1,240 ft or 378 m) is impressive – it becomes 'sharp' when viewed from beneath in Henwood village. It is disappointing to the rock climber when reached, but lengthy, easy-angled scrambles give a feeling of ascending a miniature mountain, which can be much more adventurous in rare winter snows. North again, the ridge at Bearah Tor has some short problem climbs among the rocks near the small

111

quarry. Kilmar Tor (1,299 ft or 396 m) beyond is much more impressive, its long rocky ridge offering much sport. The leaning 'Cheesewring' at the western end is a tempting ascent. Lastly, away to the north is Hawk's Tor (1,078 ft or 329 m), a fine long tor with closely-spaced horizontal joints and slabby fallen blocks. Short routes were recorded here in 1941, and more recently some very hard problems have been made. Climbing has been recorded on the north side of the much smaller Trewortha Tor. Here is also King Arthur's Bed, a curious double natural basin on the surface of one of the rocks at the west end.

Well protected modern 'sports climbing' involves great physical fitness and stamina. The climber moves up on barely visible holds on vertical and overhanging rock often taking several falls.

THE CHEESEWRING AND WILKIE COLLINS

OVER past centuries, few noteworthy writers and travellers into Cornwall failed to make a point of visiting on foot or horseback the extraordinary Cheesewring, or Wring-cheese. The Victorians were great explorers of their native island, and the novelist Wilkie Collins was one pioneer tourist who came this way on foot with his artist friend Henry Brandling in 1850. He left us valuable descriptions of a walk through the South and West Caradon Mines and his impressions of the Cheesewring itself. His book was aptly named **Rambles Beyond Railways,** for Cornwall was yet a remote corner of the kingdom. Brunel's railway from England would not cross the Tamar for another nine years, but Collins did encounter one railway – he was able to walk up the line of the Liskeard & Caradon Railway, which was then in full operation. Having visited the Trethevy Quoit, Collins and Brandling

still continued to ascend, proceeding along the tram-way leading to the Caraton Mine. Soon the scene presented another abrupt and extraordinary change. We had been walking hitherto amid almost invariable silence and solitude; but now, with each succeeding minute, strange, mingled, unintermitting noises began to grow louder and louder around us. We followed a sharp curve in the tram-way, and immediately found ourselves saluted by an entirely new prospect, and surrounded by an utterly bewildering noise. All about us monstrous wheels were turning slowly; machinery was clanking and groaning in the hoarsest discords; invisible waters were pouring onward with a rushing sound; high above our heads, on skeleton platforms, iron chains clattered fast and fiercely on iron pulleys, and huge steam pumps puffed and gasped, and slowly raised their heavy black beams of wood. Far beneath the embankment on which we stood, men, women and children were breaking and washing ore in a perfect marsh of copper-coloured mud and copper-coloured water. We had penetrated to the very centre of the noise, the bustle, and the population on the surface of a great mine. When we walked forward again, we passed through a thick plantation of young firs; and then, the sounds behind us slowly and

'The Cheese Wring near Liskeard' (J. Allen).

The Cheesewring (from an old print).

solemnly deadened the further we went on. When we had arrived at the extremity of the line of trees, they ceased softly and suddenly. It was like a change in a dream. We now left the tram-way, and stood again on the moor – on a wilder and lonelier part of it than we had yet beheld. The Cheese-Wring and its adjacent rocks were visible a mile and a half away, on the summit of a steep hill . .

On their way across the rough moors, the companions passed the Hurlers, remarking upon them at length as so many visitors had done before, and then set out towards the Cheesewring. When they got to the hill

All the granite we had seen before was as nothing compared with the granite we now looked on. The masses were at one place heaped up in great irregular cairns – at another, scattered confusedly over the ground; poured all along in close, craggy lumps; flung about hither and thither, as if in reckless sport, by the hands of giants. Above the whole rose the weird fantastic form of the Cheese-Wring, the wildest and most wondrous of all the wild and wondrous structures in the rock architecture of the scene. If a man dreamt of a great pile of stones in a nightmare, he would dream of such a pile as the Cheese-Wring. All the heaviest and largest of the seven thick slabs of which it is composed are at the top; all the lightest and smallest at the bottom . . . When you first see the Cheese-Wring, you instinctively shrink from walking under it.

Collins described the feature in detail, but just as they were admiring the solitude of the place, the two friends were greeted by three or four Liskeard drunks

flourishing porter-bottles in their hands as olive branches of peace, amity and good-will . . . One benevolent stranger held a glass in a very slanting position, while a brother philanthropist violently uncorked a bottle and directed half of its contents in a magnificent jet of light brown froth all over everybody, before he found the way into the tumbler. It was no use to decline imbibing the remainder of the light brown froth – "There was the Cheese-Wring, and here was the porter – I must drink all their good healths, and they would all drink mine – this was Cornish hospitality, and Cornish hospitality was notoriously the finest in the world!"

How different would it have been if they had encountered one of the temperance outings when many hundreds met up here, perched about the rocks – one wonders which of the two they would have preferred!

115

At last the tourists were left alone on the hill to admire the views from the summit and explore the ruins of Daniel Gumb's House. This was then the original site, and Collins gave a long account of the famous eccentric. He made no mention of the quarry, which was still in its infancy at that date. Collins and Brandling lingered here in solitude among the rocks until sunset.

Such accounts are refreshingly innocent by modern standards. Today, the greater mobility brought by motor cars and improved roads has made the Minions Moor far more accessible than in Collins's day, or even just half a century ago. The place has lost some of the remoteness felt by the author as a child in the 1950s, when 'going up to Cheesewring' from Liskeard was seen as a great adventure.

FURTHER READING

Allen, J. (1856) *History of the Borough of Liskeard and its Vicinity.*

Axford, E.C. (1975) *Bodmin Moor,* David & Charles.

Balchin, W.G.V. (1983) *The Cornish Landscape,* Hodder & Stoughton.

Barton, D. B. (1964) *A Historical Survey of The Mines and Mineral Railways of East Cornwall and West Devon,* Bradford Barton.

Barton, D.B. (1965) *The Cornish Beam Engine,* Bradford Barton.

Berry, J. (1987) *The Quarry Carvings of Bodmin Moor,* St Cleer.

Bristow, C.M. (1996) *Cornwall's Geology and Scenery: An Introduction,* Cornish Hillside Publications.

Carver, T., Stanier, P. & Littlejohn, P. (1973) *Climbing in Cornwall,* James Pike Ltd.

Collins, W. (1851) *Rambles Beyond Railways: Notes In Cornwall Taken A-Foot.*

Earl, B. (1994) *Cornish Mining,* Cornish Hillside Publications.

Edmonds, E.A., McKeown, M.C. & Williams, M. (1975) *British Regional Geology: South-West England,* HMSO.

Embrey, P.G. & Symes, R.F. (1987) *Minerals of Cornwall and Devon,* British Museum.

Gerrard, S. (1987) 'Streamworking in medieval Cornwall', *Journal of the Trevithick Society,* No.14, 7-31.

Hamilton Jenkin, A.K.H. (1966) *Mines and Miners of Cornwall. XII. Around Liskeard,* Truro Bookshop.

Hawker, R.S. (1870) *Footsteps of Former Men in Far Cornwall.*

Hawkes, C.F.C. (1983) 'The Rillaton Gold Cup', *Antiquity,* Vol LVII, 124-6.

Johnson, N. & Rose, P. (1990) *Cornwall's Archaeological Heritage,* Twelveheads Press.

Johnson, N. & Rose, P. (1994) *Bodmin Moor, an archaeological survey, Volume 1: the human landscape to c.1800,* RCHME.

Messenger, M.J. (1978), *Caradon and Looe: the Canal, Railway and Mines*, Twelveheads Press.

Sharpe, A. (1989) *The Minions Survey*, 2 volumes, Cornwall Archaeological Unit.

Stanier, P. (1985) 'Granite Working in the Cheesewring District of Bodmin Moor, Cornwall', *Journal of the Trevithick Society*, No.12, 36-49.

Stanier, P. (1986) 'Early Mining and Water Power in the Caradon Mining District of East Cornwall, *Journal of the Trevithick Society*, No.14, 32-45.

Stanier, P. (1988) *Cornwall's Mining Heritage*, Twelveheads Press.

Stanier, P. (1990) *Cornwall's Geological Heritage*, Twelveheads Press.

Thompson, E.V. (1977) *Chase the Wind*, Macmillan (a novel).

INDEX

account house 22, 38, 81
adit 40, 41, 75, 81
archaeology, 10, 56-62
barrow 15, 29-30, 57-8
beam engine
    pumping 81
    stamps 83
    winding 81
Bearah Tor 46, 53, 107, 108, 111
    quarry 46, 48, 57, 93, 99, 100
blacksmith's shop 47, 93, 99
black tin 83
boundary stones and marks 13, 20, 31, 37, 40, 43, 45-6, 47, 105-8
Bronze Age 57-61
buddle 24, 32, 83
cairn 29, 43, 45, 48, 57-8, 61
Caradon Hill 41, 43, 54, 61
Caradon Moor 36-43
Caradon Quarry 43, 100, 111
chapels 12, 74-5
Cheesewring 19, 24, 27, 53, 107-8, 111, 113-6
Cheesewring Moor 13 27
Cheesewring Quarry 15-17, 45, 51, 52, 95-100, 109-111
Clanacombe Mine 65-6
Collins, Wilkie 113-6
Cornwall Great United Mining Association 65-6, 67
cottages 22, 99, 104
Craddock Moor 28-35, 54, 60, 61, 90
Craddock Moor Circle 29, 30, 60
Craddock Moor Mine 32, 35, 69, 72
cranes 17, 43, 46, 48, 97
Crow's Nest 39, 74, 75
cultivation ridges 61
Daniel Gumb 18, 20, 101-4, 109
Daniel Gumb's House 18, 101-4, 116
Darite 73
Darley Stream Works 79, 86

dressing floors 24, 38, 40, 41, 69, 71, 83-4
drying or changing house 38
Dunsley Wheal Phoenix 80, 85
East Caradon Mine 40, 69, 72, 83, 85
elvan 51
embanked avenue 30, 60
engine houses 84
farming 31, 45, 54
felsite 51
field systems 20, 23, 30-1, 34, 45-7, 54, 60-1
flat rod 84
geology 50-2
Glasgow Caradon Consols 69, 85
Gold Diggings Quarry 22, 30, 90, 100, 111
Golitha Falls 80
Gonamena 37, 43
    incline 37, 87, 100
    Mine 37
    tinworks 43, 63
granite 50-2
    cutting 17, 97, 99
    quarrying 15-17, 95-100
    uses 17, 91, 93, 98, 100, 105
Hawk's Tor 47, 61, 112
Henwood 45, 73, 75, 111
hilltop enclosures 57
horizontal engine 85
horse whim 24, 84-5
Hurlers 13, 26, 59
hut-circle 20, 23, 30-1, 34, 45, 47, 57, 60-2
industrial archaeology 10
inns 12, 73, 75
killas 50-1
Kilmar Moor 44-49
    Railway 45-7, 87, 89, 95, 100
    Tor 46-7, 53-4, 58, 61, 93, 107-9, 111-2

119

King Doniert's Stone 61
landforms 52–5
Langstone Downs 45, 48, 54, 61
leat 38, 47, 64, 79, 85
Liskeard 73, 100
Liskeard & Caradon Railway 10, 15, 24, 37, 39–41, 61, 87–90, 95, 99, 113
lode 15, 50, 51–2, 64–5, 82, 85
long cairn 57
long houses 61
man-engine 69
Marke Valley Mine 40–2, 69, 71–2, 80
Medieval period 61–2
milestone 40, 45, 105, 107
mine names 85
minerals 51–2
mineworkers 72
mining 10, 29, 64–71, 75–86
Minions 12, 73–5, 89
    Cross 32–3, 61
    Heritage Centre 9, 24, 71
    Moor 9–10
moorstones 17–20, 91–4
Moorswater 10, 97
names 85
Neolithic period 57
North Phoenix Mine 80, 85
North Wardbrook Farm 45, 47
Oakbottom Stream Works 79, 86
Old Men 85
Pensilva 40, 73
Phoenix United Mine 22–3, 49, 51, 67, 71–2, 75, 79–80, 82
powder magazine 15, 38, 99
Prince of Wales Shaft 9, 22–3, 25, 27, 75, 77
quarry 17, 40, 47
railway 87–90
ramp 46
reservoir 24, 32, 38, 64
Rillaton Barrow 13, 15, 58
Rillaton Gold Cup 13, 15, 58–9

rock climbing 109–112
St Cleer 73, 75
shaft 24, 85–6
Sharp Tor 45–6, 49, 61, 111
Silver Valley 29, 32, 77–8
South Caradon Mine 37–9, 42, 67, 69–70, 72, 79, 84, 113
South Phoenix Mine 24, 71, 75–7
stamps 23–4, 29, 41, 64–5, 83
standing stone 13, 59, 61
stone circle 13, 26, 29–30, 59–60
stone row 30, 60
stope 82, 86
Stowe's Hill 19–22, 24, 51, 55, 93, 106, 111
Stowe's Mine 65
Stowe's Pound 20–1, 51, 57
Stowe's Shaft 22
streamworks 79, 86
tin streaming 13, 29, 32, 61, 63–4
Tokenbury Corner 39, 69
tors 46, 52–5, 111
Tregarrick Tor 30
Trethevy Quoit 57, 91, 113
Trewortha Marsh 54, 61, 63
Trewortha Tor 47, 112
turf steeds 61–2
Twelve Men's Moor 46, 54, 105
vegetation 54–5
views 20–2, 43, 45, 47
villages 73–5
water on mines 79–80
waterwheel 79–80
West Caradon Mine 38, 67, 69, 72, 113
West Phoenix Mine 31–3, 71
West Rosedown Mine 41, 69
Wheal Jenkin 41, 51, 65, 69, 77
Witheybrook 54, 61
Witheybrook Marsh 31, 62–3
Witheybrook Mine 32–3
Witheybrook tinworks 13, 31–2, 63–4

120